WE WERE
— *the* —
LAND'S

THE BIOGRAPHY OF A HOMEPLACE

JOHN HEAD

LONGSTREET
Atlanta, Georgia

Published by
LONGSTREET, INC.
A subsidiary of Cox Newspapers
A subsidiary of Cox Enterprises, Inc.
2140 Newmarket Parkway
Suite 122
Marietta, GA 30067

Printed in the United States of America

1st printing 1999

Library of Congress Catalog Card Number: 99-60105

ISBN: 1-56352-528-3

Jacket illustration: Jim Harrison
Jacket and book design by Burtch Hunter

This book is dedicated to my mother,
Myrtle Head,
who, through strength and courage, always made a way out of no way;
and to the memory of my grandmother,
Julia Fitch,
who told me stories.

WE WERE
the
LAND'S

CHAPTER 1

If fish had not fallen from the Florida sky, the Fitch
family farm might not exist. My grandmother, Julia
Fitch, told me the story of the family's flight from
Florida. She liked the place where they lived near
Jacksonville well enough. The weather was warm year-round.
She found the people she met down there to be just as warm. And
she loved to garden, so Florida's profusion of plants made it a par-
adise. But she missed the rolling hills of Middle Georgia where
she grew up; Florida's flat landscape just couldn't match it. And
she didn't like walking along a river and seeing a beast as big as a
cow swim to the surface. The first time she saw a manatee, she
told me, "It like to scared me to death."

But the unchanging terrain and even the strange creatures
grazing in the rivers did not sour her on Florida. Anyway, my
grandfather, James "Buddy" Fitch, loved Florida. He had gone
down to find work and then sent for his family to join him. Even
after the good construction jobs that drew him there dried up, he
was satisfied earning enough money for his family to survive the
Depression by helping out at a roadside vegetable stand and chas-
ing odd jobs.

To Grandma, the Depression was more ominous, something

that would only get worse. She thought the family would be better off back in Georgia where they could depend on the resources of relatives if they needed help to make it through. But she was willing to follow Grandpa's wishes and stay. She was willing until the wind blew a water spout out of the ocean, carried it over the land and dumped water—along with frantically wriggling fish— in her yard.

Some of the children—my mother included—thought it was manna from heaven, a fish fry catered by God. This was the parable of the loaves and the fishes come to life—minus the bread. My grandmother didn't think so. She saw it as a sign, and not a good one. For her, it was confirmation that Florida was a place where nature had gone haywire, and where who knew what might happen next. "Well, sir," she told me some forty years later, using the inflection of her voice to give that phrase one of its many Southern meanings, this one more or less translating into "Well, let me tell *you*. . . ."

"Well, sir," she said. "That was enough for me."

She vowed to get back to Georgia the first chance she got. That chance came when a fire destroyed the house they rented. My grandfather wanted to find another place and stay on. His dread of packing up possessions only to haul them somewhere and unpack them probably was one reason for his inertia. He always said the two hardest jobs in the world were chopping cotton and moving. Given his druthers, Grandpa said, he would rather chop cotton.

However, Grandma had other plans. "I told Poppa, 'I don't know what you're going to do, but I'm taking these children and going home.'"

In the end, my grandfather didn't put up much of a fight. He returned to Georgia and to farming, which he had grown up doing. I wonder now if this was a surrender to the fate he had been fleeing. I knew him as a reliable provider for his family, but also as a hard and joyless man. He had only one diversion I can recall—alcohol. It took him not only away from work, but from life itself.

Butts County, Georgia, was "dry" back then—meaning the selling of beer, wine, or liquor was illegal. But the creeks might as well have flowed with whiskey, the stuff was so easy to find. The local bootlegger stocked booze he bought in Atlanta and resold it with the tax stamp still intact. Or if you had less expensive tastes and a pocketbook to match, he offered Mason jars of home brew, fresh from the stills.

Sometimes Grandpa started drinking at the end of the work day on Friday and didn't stop drinking until late Saturday, giving himself time to sober up for Sunday service at Macedonia Baptist Church, where he was a deacon. He sat in "Amen Corner" with the rest of the elders, whose duties included affirming the points the preacher made during his sermon ("A man won't do right 'til he gets right with God!" "Amen!" "Won't somebody say Amen, again?" "Amen!"). The deacons also handled Macedonia's version of Catholic communion, which consisted of saltine cracker crumbs substituting for the wafers and Welch's grape juice standing in for wine. (While the county was "dry" in name only, the churches were virtual deserts when it came to alcohol.)

The rest of the week my grandfather worked from sunup to sundown five days, and sometimes six. In the country, if someone can be counted on to do his job and do it well, people say, "He's not afraid of work." Not only was Grandpa "not afraid of work," he was a predator and work was his prey. He tracked it down and attacked it, never seeming to find enough of it to satisfy his blood thirst for it. He expected everyone around him to have the same attitude. He made no exception for his children. One of my aunts told me about the time a neighbor stopped by the farm one evening and found my grandfather and his daughters working in the fields.

"Buddy, you ought not to work those children so hard," the man said.

"Why do you think I had 'em if they wasn't going to work?" Grandpa snapped.

I wonder now if he was a different, more carefree person in Florida where he wasn't rooted in the sandy soil the way he had been in the clinging red Georgia clay of the fields he plowed from his boyhood on. Or maybe Florida simply offered surer ways to make money, something he searched for throughout his life.

In any case, fish fell from the Florida sky, and he had to return to Georgia. Isn't this the way of family histories? Some unlikely or unexplainable event causes a change in course that alters everything that comes after. Those plummeting fish put my grandfather on the path to ownership of property; magic brought him and his family to the land, but it was his everyday sweat—and the sweat he squeezed from others—that watered the soil and turned the land into a farm.

Grandpa was a cash-and-carry man, hewing to the sage advice Polonius gave Laertes. He neither loaned money nor borrowed it. (I overheard him on the telephone trying to console a troubled friend. "If there's anything I can do to help," he said, "anything at all, just ask, as long as it doesn't involve money.") If he was truly strapped for cash himself, he simply sold some of his land. It would be easy to fault my grandfather and those like him for allowing land to slip away through attrition. But the alternative was to go into debt. And Grandpa had seen enough farms sold on the courthouse steps and families forced out of homes with nothing to take with them to believe debt meant ruination.

So the property went, like pieces taken one at a time out of a puzzle. By the time my grandmother died—fifty years after the land was purchased—only a fraction remained to be handed over to a second generation. It appeared they would be the last in our family to lay claim to the land. There were almost twenty heirs when the surviving siblings and the children of those who had passed on were totaled. They owned the property together, and they fought about it as only family members can fight—with even the smallest matters made large by past hurts that endure among people held close by kinship ties forged in familial love, ties so strong that they hold people fast even when love has long faded. They discussed and argued and refused to talk about it until the last of them was worn down and submitted to the logic of selling the place.

With that decision the chain of ownership could have ended. But then, for reasons I did not completely understand, I decided to buy this rundown, overgrown, used-to-be-a-farm. I talked my brother James, an attorney out in California, into joining me. We knew we could keep the land in the family for a third generation. We hoped to turn it into something that could be passed down to all generations to come.

+≔ ≔+

A piece of family lore held that my grandfather got someone from "the white side" of the family to take out the mortgage to buy the land, because banks back then wouldn't loan money to a black man. It's a plausible story. Grandpa was light-skinned. He had cousins who were so light they could pass for white. There's no doubt that there was white blood in the family, with a little Creek Indian mixed in, too. As for the bank, no one who knows the history of the rural South would be surprised that a black man looking to buy land couldn't get a loan from the local bank.

But the story apparently is not true. A title search showed that in 1939, one James Fitch paid two thousand dollars cash for 103 acres of Butts County, Georgia, land from the McCords, a prominent white family. There is no mention of any loan or mortgage middleman. There also is no mention of where my grandfather—who, as far as I can determine, had not gotten rich working odd jobs in Florida—got two thousand dollars cash in the depths of the Great Depression.

A mysterious transaction took place fifteen years after Grandpa bought the land. According to a second deed that surfaced in the title search, Lewis H. Cawthon sold six acres of that same land—and the house that had been built on it—to my grandfather. The price the second time around was "One dollar and other considerations."

Getting six acres and a house for one dollar is a bargain by any reckoning. But why would anyone—particularly someone with Grandpa's ferocious frugality—pay even that token amount for property he already owned? And what were those "other considerations?"

The document did contain this sentence: "This deed is made for the purpose of verifying the land line between grantor and grantee." What land line? I studied the original deed from my grandfather's purchase. It listed the owners of property that bordered the land he bought. There was not a Cawthon among them. And I knew from my childhood memories that Grandpa farmed much more than six acres of land around the house well after 1954.

When I asked my mother and my aunts and uncles about how Grandpa got the land, they said he bought all 103 acres from one of the Cawthon brothers. Mom said she heard stories that Grandpa bought all the land for one dollar. Might there be a grain of truth in that family lore after all? Did Grandpa own the property outright as the first deed indicated, or was Lewis Cawthon secretly involved for "other considerations" that would take my grandfather fifteen years to repay? Was there something between the two, something that couldn't be recorded on paper?

When I wrote about my puzzlement over this in the *Atlanta Constitution*, the newspaper I work for, a colleague walked up to me and said the answer was plain.

"I can't believe you've become such a big-city boy that you can't figure out what was going on there," Jim Wooten said. Like me, he is a son of the rural, small-town South, so he was entitled to tease me. "Obviously, your grandfather was working the land for this other fella. They must have had some kind of sharecropping arrangement."

If this was sharecropping, it certainly wasn't a typical example. Sharecropping replaced slavery in the South after Emancipation. Some say it was like slavery, only worse. A slave didn't get paid for working; a sharecropper had to pay someone to let him work. The sharecropper (almost always black) was allowed to plant cotton on the land of another man (*always* white) in exchange for handing over a portion of the crop. In addition to housing, the landowner usually provided food and other supplies, with his costs to be covered in the division of the crop.

The problem for the sharecropper was that if the crop was poor or failed altogether, he was in debt to the landowner. Some found themselves in debt by the landowner's accounting even when they produced bumper crops. The debt could grow deeper and deeper each year, until a sharecropper had no hope of digging himself out. On top of that, the sharecropper was on the land at the pleasure of the man who owned the property. That man was lord of the land in every sense that the word "landlord" conveys. If the landowner was displeased for any reason, he could order the sharecropper to leave.

My grandfather's situation appeared to be nothing like that—not even close. He had title to the land. If he didn't really own it, why go through an elaborate ruse to make it appear that he did? Was this some enlightened version of that instrument of racial oppression called sharecropping?

I doubt that. As far as I know, Butts County was no incubator of racial harmony half a century ago. It wasn't the worst place in the South for race relations, but it wasn't close to the best, either. Donald Grant, in *The Way Things Were in the South*, his history of black people in Georgia, recounts the lynching of Henry Etheridge near Jackson, the county seat. Etheridge's offense was promoting the back-to-Africa movement among blacks in Butts County. I know of at least one lynching that took place while I was growing up in the county, and of an incident in which night riders—the Ku Klux Klan enforcers who, under cover of darkness, terrorized "trouble-making" blacks—fired shots into the home of a local civil rights leader.

Such history only raises more questions about how my grandfather got the land and what it meant for him to own it. Why was any white man willing to sell that much land to a black man? What did other people in the community—black and white— think of it? If the resale really was about a property line dispute, why didn't Lewis Cawthon, who certainly occupied a superior status compared to Grandpa, simply declare that the line was where he said it was and that was that?

My list of questions grows. But even as new queries are added and my chain of questions lengthens link by link, the dilemma is always this: When so many of these mysteries can be resolved only by knowing what was in the hearts and minds of the people now dead, where do I find the answers? My grandfather, a man of few words when he was living, has been dead for thirty years. Grandma told me stories, but she didn't have time to tell and I didn't have time to listen to all the stories I now wish I knew.

＋⊶　⊷＋

Houses and farmland once were living things. They were not merely built or bought; they were born. And, like babies, they took on the traits of those for whom they were born or of those who adopted them. My grandparents put parts of their innermost selves into the only house and land they would ever own. They embued the property with essences of themselves the way parents pass their genes to their children.

My grandfather gave the house its utilitarian toughness. It was unspectacular but sturdy, made to stand up under the burden of their children. There were six children at home then—five girls (my mother Myrtle, Bessie, Marie, Helen, and Doris) and a boy, Marvin, who was the youngest. The four oldest boys (James, Randolf, Fred, and Chester) had crossed over into manhood and were out on their own. They soon would be off to soldier in World War II.

As the years passed, the farm became a way station for my grandparents' children and an ever-growing cadre of grandchildren. There were no frills; every feature was plain and functional. The house was all straight lines and sharp angles, like my grandfather's face, and it was long and narrow, like his lanky frame. Unadorned, the rooms were as spare as an empty packing crate. There was nothing distinctive about it, except that it was one of the few two-story farmhouses in the county. But even that was a matter of function rather than style. You have more house taking up less land that way.

The house inherited my grandmother's gentle generosity. She cooked constantly, so the house always smelled as if company was coming. She made the lace curtains that fluttered slowly in the windows, like the wings of resting butterflies. She softened the angles with simple things of beauty—a sea shell, an egg-shaped polished stone, a ball of crystal glass.

Likewise, my grandparents tried to shape the land the way they shaped their lives. For my grandfather, it was all about clearing and plowing and squeezing as much value out of it as possible. Just as he saw his children as units of labor, he measured the land in bales of cotton per acre and bushels of corn and sweet potatoes.

The land was not only alive; it was teeming with life. Grandpa spent most of his time competing with those other living things to stake his claim. He fought adversaries of all kinds, enemies that flew, walked, crept, hopped, or burrowed in to eat his crops. And there were enemies that grew up out of the ground and sur-rounded his plants, choking them or sucking the nutrients they needed out of the soil. Grandpa was the stern disciplinarian to his unruly 103 acres. He believed in letting them know who was boss. Once he got the land to bend to his will, he used an iron fist to keep it in line.

My grandmother, on the other hand, caressed the land with her fingers and used that loving touch to convince it to yield gar-dens of fragrant beauty. (Having thought about my grandparents' differing approaches to the land, I now can imagine Grandma standing with hands on hips and telling some recalcitrant flower, "You just wait 'til your father gets home!") She grew rose of Sharon, four o'clocks, forsythia, morning glory, sunflowers, and roses of various sizes and colors. She tended and picked from apple trees, a pear tree, and a peach tree. And there were black-berry bushes that needed no tending. They gave fruit to anyone with the courage to confront their thorns in order to pick enough for pies and preserves.

Grandma's green thumb provided me with more than an

appreciation for the beauty and bounty of plants. It allowed me to learn the value of showing contrition after committing a crime and of showing a willingness to accept the proper punishment. The yard was full of shrubs and bushes of various kinds. We knew when we had committed that rare transgression that placed us beyond even Grandma's forgiveness.

"Go get me a switch," she told us, and we went searching for the instrument of our own corporal comeuppance. The trick was to come up with a switch that fit the crime. Return with one that was too small, and Grandma, exasperated, would go find one large enough to increase the penalty to cover the added charge of attempting to obstruct justice.

Those are some of the broad memories of my grandparents' house and land. I took such visions with me to a local bank on that February day when my brother James—who had come all the way from California—and I signed the papers to buy the farm. The bank president welcomed us into his office before the closing. He talked about how much he enjoyed working on civic projects with my brother Fred, the first African American elected to the Butts County Commission. Later, one of the loan officers asked us if we had seen Fred's wife, Brenda, who was the first black branch manager for the bank. Whether or not the story about his being unable to get a bank loan was true, Grandpa would be amazed at what took place in that bank that day. He would be amazed at the changes that had taken place in Butts County, not just in the almost sixty years since he bought the land in 1939, but also in the twenty-nine years since his death in 1968.

He might have been even more amazed at the price his grandsons paid for the tiny puzzle piece that remained of the land he bought—along with the house he paid to have built on it—and the debt we took on to buy it. Grandpa paid two thousand dollars for 103 acres. I have no idea what the house cost. But the house and land together couldn't have cost him a fraction of the forty-three thousand dollars we paid for them on February 18, 1997. And the thirty-three-thousand-dollar mortgage we took out had to be more debt than he accumulated in his entire life. In fact, I would bet the debt I ran up within one month of getting my first credit card was more than he owed in his lifetime.

A few days after the closing, when I knew the tenants who were living there would be away, I went to the farmhouse. I wanted to know how it would feel to stand there as the owner of my childhood dreams, which is what the farm had become.

The lyrics of one of my favorite songs came to me as I walked up the front porch steps. It's a Jackson Browne song about someone who "looked into a house I once lived in" to "see where my beginnings had gone." I wondered at that moment if looking back was what buying the farm was about. Was I trying to see where I had come from in order to figure out where I ought to be going? This was more than a renovation project. I knew that. What lay ahead was the reconstruction of memories—memories of this place and the people who were here before me.

Yes, the house and the land are living things. They have stories to tell, if only we know how to listen. Standing on the front porch that day, I knew this place no longer felt like the place I had known. I didn't believe I could re-create that place, but I hoped to rediscover it. I wanted the stories of the Fitch family farm to unfold day by day, answering all those questions I had never even known to ask. I wanted to be immersed in the long-buried details. In the end, I wanted my work on the house and the land to provide enough revelations to write the biography of this family place.

CHAPTER 2

From the second floor I look down the dark stairway and see all the way back to my earliest memory. I don't know how old I was. I was a toddler. Perhaps I had just started walking.

I remember it clearly, though. I thought I would fall forever if I tried to walk down the stairs. Each step looked like a sheer cliff at oblivion's edge. But I needed to get downstairs, and there was no one to carry me. So I turned around and eased my way down the stairway backwards, like a mountain climber descending from the summit.

Now as I look down, the distance to the first floor is not very far, and the stairs that take you there are not that steep. Much of the house has performed the same shrinking act when measured against my memory. It's early June, not long after I saw the inside of the farmhouse for the first time in years. I had forgotten how the house looked to me as an adult. My childhood memories were much clearer. But the spacious, light-filled rooms that I recall are replaced by small, cramped, dark rooms. It's hard to imagine more than a handful of people inside the living room where my grandparents, my three brothers and my sister, an aunt and uncle, a few cousins, and I gathered at night to listen to the radio or, eventually, to watch television. In the kitchen-dining room where Grandma seemed to always have something cooking, there is barely enough room to turn around. The upstairs bedroom I shared with my three brothers, along with whichever out-of-town cousins who were visiting, is smaller than any bedroom of any of the apartments I've ever rented—and I have rented some tiny apartments. The whole house has about twelve hundred feet of living space, including the single bathroom, added after I went away to college.

Getting inside the house to size it up was not easy. Removing the tenants who were renting when we bought it was not as simple as I'd hoped. Charlie Greer was there with his daughter and what seemed to be a constantly changing cast of grandchildren. When the heirs decided to sell the house, my mother told Mr. Greer that James and I probably would buy it. I went to the house one Saturday in December to look around outside. Mr. Greer walked with me, and at every opportunity he pointed out something he had done to "improve" the property: cut down a huge dying tree in the back (most of it still lying on the ground, being rapidly consumed by kudzu), kept the grass trimmed, demolished a dilapidated storage shed. "We been here for three years," he said, "and I always treated the place like it was my own."

But it isn't yours, I thought. I didn't speak that bluntly. Instead, I said James and I were going to buy the house, probably around the first of the year. We planned to do major restoration work that would require that the house be empty. I told him my mother had offered to help him find another place. His only reply was to look out over the land, nod his head, and say, "All right."

We closed on the house on February 18. I told Mr. Greer I wanted to start work by the middle of April, giving him sixty days' notice to vacate. He said that was plenty of time. The lawyer in James wanted to get his agreement to leave in writing, or, at the very least, for us to notify him in writing of the exact date by which he had to leave. I thought that wasn't necessary. "Mom is helping them to find another place to rent," I said. "They'll be long gone by April."

I was wrong. February turned into March and March into April, and there still was no sign that the Greers planned to move. I asked Mom what was going on. She said she found several rental possibilities, but either the Greers decided it wasn't the place they wanted to rent or the owners decided the Greers were not the tenants they wanted. At one point, the Greers made an offer to buy a house, but that fell through.

It was almost May when I made another Saturday trip to see Mr. Greer. I didn't like doing it. I felt like some absentee land-lord coming down from Atlanta telling a family to get out. Never in my life did I ever think I'd be on this side of the age-old property battle. I found Mr. Greer on the back porch steps, having a beer and enjoying the sunshine. The pleasantries were perfunctory. "I really want to get started working on the house," I said. "I need to have some contractors come in and make bids."

"Yes sir, I know," he said. "You been real nice to let us stay on this long. We're going to be outta here real soon."

"Do you know when?"

"Oh, we can be gone real soon. Just tell us when you want us out."

How about last week? I thought. Instead, I asked, "When's the soonest you think you can move?"

"We could move next week if things fall right. I got a little check coming in. Then we can get up enough to pay you the last month's rent and put a deposit down on another place."

"Don't worry about the last month's rent," I said. "Just put it toward the deposit."

"Yes sir," he said. "I appreciate that. You been real nice to us. When I get that check next week I'll go make that deposit and we'll be gone. I can promise you that."

I left the farm furious both at Charlie Greer and at myself. He had used against me a kind of stereotypical black survival skill. He treated me with an undue deference bordering on affection, even though he was old enough to be my father and must have hated what he surely saw as my callous treatment of him. He told me what I wanted to hear, as if he could read my mind.

And that made me the landlord ordering the sharecropper and his family off my land. I didn't like playing the villain, even though I felt I had no choice. But I wondered how many landowners told themselves they had no choice but to throw a man and his family out into the world with no place to go. Who was more justified, the landowner who made decisions based on who would give him the most value out of his land and the least trouble, or me, the guy who was putting a family out because of some vague notion of keeping the land in the family and turning the farm back into the place he remembered? What was my hurry? Couldn't I let them stay on as tenants for as long as they needed? Perhaps I could let them stay while the renovation work was going on.

No, I thought. I'm an owner of the land. That's important to me, but not just for the sake of ownership. That's not even what's most important. Robert Frost wrote, "We were the land's before the land was ours." For the descendants of slaves, those words speak literal truth rather than take poetic license. The Africans brought here weren't just slaves to masters; they also were slaves to the land. The land made them valuable. The land paid for them. And for families like mine, the land bound them together through generations.

I decided I wasn't the villain in this piece. I had given the Greers more than adequate notice. They couldn't stay during the renovation. Even walking around outside the house it was evident that a great deal of work needed to be done. I made a list of the things that probably needed fixing (new wiring and plumbing, for example) and totaled what it might cost to do it. I tried to err on the side of overestimation. I wanted to be as pessimistic as possible so I wouldn't be disappointed. I soon discovered, however, that, if anything, I was being wildly optimistic.

+=━ ━=+

I drove into downtown Jackson. The county seat is still a small town, but larger than it was during my childhood. Like most small Southern towns that are more than a few buildings along a short stretch of highway, that are large enough to have a traffic light, Jackson's business district revolves around the county courthouse, which, with the requisite Confederate memorial prominent on the courthouse square, remains the most imposing building downtown.

The malling of America has hit Jackson the same way it has hit towns throughout the country. People are drawn to the shiny new shopping centers like metal filings to a magnet. The local five-and-dime store and the downtown family grocery store are long gone. Other businesses have tried to adapt by offering new services—there's a video rental store now—and by emphasizing the convenience of "shopping at home." Following the custom of the small-town South, downtown Jackson would shut down on Wednesdays, giving merchants a day off to compensate for being open on Saturday, the largest shopping day when people came in from the country to stock up. There were two drugstores, and they took turns being open on Wednesday to make sure people had a place to get emergency prescriptions filled. These days, Wednesday is just another work day downtown, another day for bringing in enough money to hang on.

County government must have grown lately. All the county agencies once were housed in the courthouse. Now some have been parceled out to annexes in the converted buildings of closed businesses. The County Water and Sewer Authority is one of these. I went there to get the account placed in my name, my first stamp of ownership of the farm, other than signing my name to the mortgage papers.

The woman behind the counter went to a computer and pulled up the account for the farm. In much less time than it took me to draw a bucket of water from the well when I was a child, she had wiped the Greers from the account and made me responsible for paying the water bill. She turned to one of her coworkers. "Do you know where Johnny is?" she asked. "He's out there somewhere," the woman replied. "I'd try to get him on the radio."

The first woman turned back to me. "Are you going to be out there for a while?" she asked.

"I'll be out there the rest of the day."

"Well, we'll find Johnny and send him out to turn the water on. He should be out there in about fifteen minutes."

Yeah, right, I thought. If any government worker could get anywhere in fifteen minutes, I hadn't met him. I drove back to the farm expecting to spend most of the rest of the day waiting.

Ten minutes after I got back to the farm, a Butts County Water & Sewer Authority truck turned into the driveway. Johnny was very tall and very skinny, with blond hair and what looked like a teenager's peach fuzz on his face. The first words he said as he walked toward me in the front yard were, "Do you know of anybody that looks after birds?"

I wasn't sure I heard him correctly. "What?" I said.

"Do you know of anybody that looks after birds?" he repeated. "I found a hurt blackbird laying in the road on the way over here. I got him in the truck and I want to take him to somebody who can take care of him."

"No," I said. "I don't know of anyone."

Johnny extended his hand. "You Mr. Head?" he said.

"That's right," I said as we shook hands.

He looked toward the house. "You renting it?"

"No, I just bought it. Right now, I'm coming down from Atlanta to do some repair work on it. After that's done we'll see what to do with it."

Johnny's eyes sparked with interest. "You from Atlanta?" he said. "What church you belong to up there?"

The question took me aback. Somewhat flustered, I said, "Oh, I'm still a member of Macedonia Baptist down here." That was true, even though I had been inside the church maybe once in the past twenty years.

"I been going to First Street Baptist over in Griffin," he said. "It's really been a blessing. You can feel the Spirit is strong there."

I passed on my chance to keep the conversation going. After a few moments of silence, Johnny said, "Let's get you turned on."

And so, within twenty minutes of asking that the water be turned on, the water was on. That was accomplished despite the water department employee's having stopped to pick up an injured bird and spending a few minutes talking to me about religion, with no apparent concern that I might object to proselytizing by a government employee as a violation of the separation of church and state. "You're not in Atlanta anymore, John," I said to myself.

+➤═ ═◄+

It wasn't until I started destroying the house that I began to realize how much work was needed to save it. Gutting the interior had been in the plan from the beginning. There was no way to avoid putting in new plumbing and wiring, as well as insulation. That meant opening the walls. I could do that kind of unskilled labor and save money I would otherwise pay a plumber and electrician. So I bought a pry bar and a crowbar and began laying bare the house's soul.

The walls and ceilings were made of tongue-and-groove boards. In downstairs rooms, the wood had been covered with Sheetrock. Upstairs, where I started the demolition in heat that already was sweltering in mid-spring, the wood was either exposed or covered only by wallpaper so old and fragile that it crumbled if touched. Movement of the house over the years had caused gaps between some of the tight-fitting boards, and some nails had worked their way a fraction of an inch out of the wood into which they had been hammered almost sixty years ago. This made the job of prying out the boards a little easier, but it was still difficult, exhausting work. The coveralls I wore were always soaked with sweat an hour after I began the job.

My work disturbed decades of dust, especially when I pulled boards from the ceilings. I had to wear a dust mask, which made me look like a surgeon. My operation on the house wasn't performed with surgical precision, however. Initially, I removed all the boards carefully, trying to do as little damage as possible. I wanted to save the wood for reuse, perhaps as flooring or for cabinets. The idea of recycling the wood and giving new life to this original part of the house appealed to me. But it was tedious work, and I discovered water and termite damage on the inside of much of the wood once I took it down. I decided to reserve gentle removal for the wood of the "indoors" walls; for the rest, I ripped the boards out quickly, unconcerned that brute force would leave them splintered or broken.

The house soon began revealing secrets it had kept inside itself for years. Nests of the wasps we called dirt daubers clung to studs inside the walls, forming insect adobe villages. There also were nests of generations of birds that found openings in the siding and returned to the house spring after spring to lay eggs and raise their broods. Fresh layers were added to the nests over the years, until the straw and sticks and bits of paper were piled from floor to ceiling. I also found the nests of mice, along with the complete skeletons of their final inhabitants. I was an archaeologist, uncovering the ruins of tiny civilizations.

What really intrigued me, though, was the evidence of human habitation, the strange variety of manmade artifacts I discovered inside the walls and the ceiling. I found coins (some dated in the 1960s), toys, a knife and fork, small bottles, and other articles of everyday life. How did they get inside a wall or ceiling? Were they like a splinter that enters someone's foot and over the years works its way to other parts of the body? They were in places it seemed unlikely anyone would have lost them.

One day, as I took boards from a ceiling, a piece of paper fluttered down in a cloud of dust. It was a page from a Bible, turned brown over the years. I picked it up carefully, wondering if this was some divine message sent to guide me. Once I read the page, though, I decided it wasn't relevant to what I was doing. At least, I hoped it wasn't relevant. If this was a prophecy of how things would go with the house, I was in big trouble.

The page included verses from the first three chapters of the Book of Habakkuk. The prophet complains of the violence he has suffered, and how his attackers go unpunished. *O Lord, how long shall I cry, and thou wilt not hear! even cry out unto thee of violence, and thou wilt not save!* Habakkuk laments. *Why dost thou shew me iniquity, and cause me to behold grievance? for spoiling and violence are before me: and there are that raise up strife and contention. Therefore the law is slacked, and judgment dost not go forth: for the wicked doth compass about the righteous; therefore wrong judgment proceedeth.*

Well. Perhaps this biblical tale of evil triumphant miraculously slipped through an invisible crack and waited in the ceiling for years for me to find it, but it did not contain any sign from God I wanted to heed. So I chose to ignore it. Besides, my attention was diverted from signs to a signature.

I found the handwriting *inside* the wall when I pried down tongue-and-groove boards in a corner of one of the back bedrooms upstairs. It was scrawled along what was probably the final piece of siding nailed to the house. Was this the finishing touch of a craftsman who signed his work as an artist signs a painting?

The signature was difficult to decipher. The initial definitely was a "G." But the last name could have been "Mathews" or "Mathborn" or "Mashburn" or any variation thereof. Or the "M" might actually have been a "W." Then and there, I committed myself to deciphering the signature and finding out who this mystery man was.

Later, I found more names. They were downstairs, inside the kitchen walls. Men called Tweet, Rip, George, and Obe (unless a member of the Order of the British Empire stopped by while the house was being built) had printed their names for posterity. I assumed "George" was the man upstairs—Mr. M—and the others were the crew working for him. Knowing the boss was the key to opening more of the house's secrets.

Figuring out his name would only be a start. I probably could identify Mr. M with some elementary detective work—check courthouse records or simply ask around about carpenters who worked in the area in the early 1940s. There still might be people around who remember the man with the M-name who built Buddy Fitch's house on Covington Highway. But I wanted more than I could get from faded official documents or the recesses of someone's memory, however deep. I didn't just want to know the man's name. I wanted to know the man. I wanted to know him because that would help me know the house he built.

I wanted to learn if he was good at his work, if he enjoyed doing it. Was he someone people could count on, someone who wasn't afraid of work? Did he show up on the job as soon as there was enough light to see, or did people squint down the road into the afternoon sun hoping to see him coming at last, and wondering whether it was time to go looking for him? Was that signature inside the wall a sign of pride in his work, or nothing more than graffiti left to show that he had been there? As a practical matter, if I could know what kind of man Mr. M was, I could know what kind of house he built, and I could better judge its strengths and weaknesses. And that knowledge might make a difference in how I approached restoration of the house.

I wonder if Mr. M would have improved his penmanship if he had known that almost sixty years later so much would depend on the grandson of his employer knowing exactly who he was.

<hr>

I know I did this backwards. The smart homebuyer gets the house inspected before putting his money down. It's best to know what problems you're buying, after all. That's why it's said you should never buy a house because you've fallen in love with it. Love is blind, but you'd better have your eyes open for evidence of the leaky roof, the flooding basement, the gnawing termites, or any other potential catastrophes hiding in houses.

But this was not about smart home-buying. It was about love. My love for this place was born in my childhood. There was no need to have the house inspected first. No discovery, no matter how damaging, would have dissuaded me.

I asked Dan Curl to do the inspection for me. Years before, someone had recommended Dan to me for another inspection job. I never got in touch with him about that, but I eventually met him on the tennis court, where he was both an elegant and tenacious player. We played fairly regularly for a while. Dan always won.

I hadn't seen Dan for a while when I called him about inspecting the farmhouse. He had been diagnosed with cancer the year before and had undergone chemotherapy. The treatment left him too weak to play tennis. He talked easily about his illness as we rode in my truck toward Jackson.

"I'm feeling stronger," Dan said. "I'm almost to the point where I'm ready to start playing again. I've been working with the weights, trying to get some muscle tone back. But I go out on the court to hit some balls and the stamina just isn't quite there.

"I just try to take things one step at a time and not rush to do things. One thing having cancer has taught me is to be patient, not to try to do it all at once."

I just listened. I didn't say what I was thinking, which was that it seemed to me that a life-threatening illness would teach you to do as much as you can while you can, to hurry up, not slow down, because you never really know how long you have left. But the next moment I thought how foolish and self-centered I was being. Dan was the one who was suffering through the illness and fighting it. He's entitled to draw his own lessons from it without me offering my interpretation, which was completely uninformed by experience.

By the time we arrived in Jackson, the topic of conversation had shifted from Dan to me. He looked around as we drove through town. "So, why did you buy your grandparents' farm?" he asked. "Are you getting sentimental over your hometown?"

There's that question again. Why? Sentimentality over Jackson is not the answer. There's not that much left to be sentimental about here. Except for the short stretch through the heart of downtown, Jackson's main drag looks like a strip of road in suburbia, only on a smaller scale. Dan and I drove past a McDonald's, a Burger King, a Pizza Hut, a Chinese restaurant, a Kentucky Fried Chicken, three stop-and-shop gas station/convenience stores, a Piggly Wiggly grocery store, and several other businesses that were not there when I grew up in Jackson.

Thomas Wolfe's literary warning that you can never go home again isn't merely about whether the people back home will accept you. It's also about whether "home" will still be there waiting for you. The Jackson, Georgia, I knew isn't there any more. It isn't just a superficial transformation brought on by the arrival of McDonald's and other franchises that make the town look a lot like every other town. It goes deeper than that. A drug house flourished across the street from my mother's house for months until the police finally busted it and the city boarded it up. Jackson was in the news recently as the center of an auto insurance scam, with several local residents arrested. The town is changing with the times, and so are the people.

"No, I don't think it's sentiment," I said to Dan. "I just thought it was important to keep the place in the family." But even as I spoke those words, I knew there was more to it than that.

━━ ━━

Dan Curl grabbed a flashlight, ready to probe dark and dusty places in order to tell me how to save the house. As we walked through and around the house he conducted a serious conversation with a micro-recorder, while addressing me in mostly light-hearted asides.

"Electrical panel is not up to standard, with main lines exposed. Recommend replacement," he said into the recorder, before turning to me and adding, "Wow, this thing is old. It must have been one of the first switch boxes invented." (The phrases "not up to standard" and "recommend replacement" were repeated so many times that day, they might as well have been refrains from disco songs.)

"The house has a metal roof with extensive rusting," Dan told the recorder as we stood in the middle of a field and he peered at the roof through a pair of small binoculars. Noting patches of black amid the rust-brown, he said, "Repair patches indicate leaks in the past." Then, speaking to me as he continued to look through the binoculars, Dan said, "It may not look too good, but a tin roof can last forever. I'll bet we'll find some water damage but probably not a lot and probably not recent." When inside inspection confirmed his prediction, Dan turned to me and said, "Am I good, or what?" He reminded me of a doctor with a good bedside manner making his rounds at a hospital: Tell the patients what's wrong, but be positive when you can. And don't take everything too seriously, especially yourself.

When we went upstairs, Dan noticed I had started prying the tongue-and-groove boards from the walls. "You don't see walls like this anymore," he said. "Why are you taking them down?"

"I want to put up Sheetrock," I said.

"You can Sheetrock over them."

"I'm also going to put in insulation."

"You can leave them up and have insulation blown in," Dan insisted. "I just wouldn't take them down. They add to the structural soundness of the house."

Dan moved to the middle of the main bedroom, jumped up and stomped down with both feet several times. He held the recorder close to his lips. "There's definite sloping of the floor from the center joist to the outside edges of the room. But there's little floor vibration."

"Houses settle over the years," Dan told me. "I wouldn't worry too much about this unless we find something else."

That "something else" was waiting for us downstairs in the kitchen. That barely noticeable gradual slope in the floor upstairs was more like a severe drop-off from the kitchen toward the back of the house. There was obvious water damage around the sink. Tin, plywood, and particleboard had been nailed down to cover holes in the floor. Dan didn't bother to jump up and down to test for structural soundness. He might have gone right through if he tried that in the wrong place.

"There's water damage here, but I'm afraid there might be more than that going on," Dan said as he kneeled down and

looked under the sink. "It's not just a leak from the pipes. It looks
like the whole floor is involved."

It was worse in the bathroom. Daylight came through the wall
near the base of the toilet. The floor was covered with some kind
of veneer paneling. It felt spongy with each step. There was a gap
in the floor running along the bathtub. It was hard to say what
law of physics held the tub in place. "Geez," was about all Dan
had to say.

We walked around to the back of the house. Something
stopped Dan in this tracks. "Look at that," he said.

"Look at what?" I asked.

"That pipe running up the side of the house. It's the sewer
vent pipe. It allows sewer gases to escape. Look at how it stops
right at that bedroom window on the second floor. If the window is open, the gases will be vented into that room. That's not
only a code violation; it's downright dangerous."

Dan looked up and down the pipe. He shook his head a few
more times before we crawled under the house to get a better
look at the floor damage. Dan shone his flashlight from spot to
spot, again shaking his head. "You've got major problems here,"
he said. "Major structural problems. Looks like someone tried to
make repairs, but I don't see that they did much good. Look at
this joist they added here. It's not providing any support. It's sort
of just hanging there. And these two-by-fours they used as connectors between the bad joists? What are those for? They don't
do a thing as far as fixing the problem goes. And look at the way
somebody nailed new wood to the rotten wood back there. That
makes no sense."

Dan was working himself toward indignation over the shoddy
work. "This is actually dangerous," he said. "I wouldn't fill that
tub with water, much less get into it. It's going to come through
the floor one day."

There was more head shaking, almost sorrowfully this time.
"You need to get a structural guy in here to take a look," Dan
said. "I know you've got a lot of water damage, lots of rot. And
there's evidence of termite activity. That main beam over there is

pretty much gone. Somebody can take a close look and tell you what can be done to fix it. But I'd guess you're looking at jacking up the house and doing foundation work. You can really get into some money doing that."

The day had turned even more dreary by the time we crawled from under the house. The drizzle was heavier, the sky grayer. "Well," I said to Dan, "what do you think I should do? Is it worth putting the work into it?"

"That's up to you, John. The house was what your grandfather wanted it to be. It served the purpose he intended for it. But, basically, it's just a big old barn of a house. If you want to make it into something else and bring it up to today's standards, it's going to take time and money to do it. You're the only one who knows what that's worth to you, how much you're willing to spend on it."

That answer made me uneasy. It didn't matter much what Dan thought. I was already set on restoring the house. I really shouldn't have asked the question. But having asked it, I felt compelled to press on. "Dan, I'd just like to know what you'd do in my place. What would you do if this was your house?"

"It's not my house, John."

"I just want your professional opinion, Dan. I'm not putting the rest of my life in your hands. I'll consider what you say, but the decision is going to be mine, not yours."

Dan hesitated, and then he looked away. He looked like the upbeat doctor who finally had to face the family of a patient who was not going to get better—ever. He turned back and looked me in the eye. Then I realized that what he had to say was even worse than I thought. I had seen him talking into the recorder like a doctor making a diagnosis, trying to gather enough information about the patient's illness to prescribe a cure. Perhaps things started that way. At some point, however, the doctor making a diagnosis became the coroner conducting an autopsy.

"If this was my house," Dan said, "I'd tear it down."

CHAPTER 3

D an Curl pulled his punches in person, but not on paper. The summary of his inspection of the farmhouse was as direct as a Muhammad Ali left jab, and just as stinging.

OPINION: *NO DISTINCTIVE ARCHITECTURAL DETAIL OR DESIGN IS PRESENT,* Dan wrote. *THE EXTENT OF REPAIRS NEEDED TO ACHIEVE CURRENT FUNCTION AND SAFETY DESIGN STANDARDS DOES NOT WARRANT RENOVATION.*

Nothing distinctive about it at all, I thought bitterly, except that it was the first and only house my grandparents ever owned, the place from which they sent their children—including my mother—out into the world.

But I really had no reason to be angry. I asked Dan to be honest with me. He was. The physician analogy is apt again. A doctor who tells you that someone you love has a life-threatening illness hasn't caused the disease. A doctor who lies and says everything is fine hasn't cured it. Dan told me that everything was not well with the house, and he gave me the prescription for treating its ills.

1. FRAMING REPAIRS AT THE BATHROOM, KITCHEN, AND REAR PORCH.

2. COMPLETE REWORKING OF MECHANICAL SYSTEMS (HEAT AND A/C, PLUMBING, AND ELECTRIC), INCLUDING DESIGN.

3. NEAR-TERM REPLACEMENT OF ROOFING.

4. WINDOW REPLACEMENT, INCLUDING SILLS.

5. REMOVAL OF VINYL SIDING AND REPAIRS/REPLACEMENT OF WOOD SIDING AS NEEDED.

6. REAR PORCH REMOVAL AND RECONSTRUCTION.

7. INTERIOR REPAIRS, INCLUDING: FLOORING, WALLS, CABINETS/STORAGE, ANY DESIRED FLOOR PLAN CHANGES, AND INTERIOR DOORS.

8. REVIEW OF SEPTIC SYSTEM.

9. ENERGY DESIGN, INSULATION.

Other than that, the place was in mint condition.

While Dan gave no encouragement to my dream of restoring the house, he was cautious in his pessimism. His recommendation didn't mention the potential problems with the foundation, even though that was what Dan was most worried about during the inspection. I'm sure there are times when doctors in general practice are relieved that their training limits just how definitive they can be in diagnosing the most devastating illnesses. Much like the family doctor, Dan was leaving the job of delivering the really bad news to a specialist.

Dan also tried to gently inject a little realism into my dream when I told him I hoped to do most of the restoration work myself. "For a job like that, you need to know what you're doing," Dan said. "I'm not saying you can't do it. You'd just be better off at least having advice from a contractor. The best thing would be to spend two or three years apprenticing with somebody. Then you'd be qualified to do it all yourself."

"I don't want to take two or three years, Dan. I'd like to have it done by the end of this year. I think I can."

"What's your hurry?" Dan asked. "It's not like you don't have any place to live and have to move into this house as soon as possible. You've got to have some patience."

But I didn't have much patience. I wanted to get the job done as quickly as possible. The first step was to find someone who could keep the house from falling down around me.

Looking for a contractor to work on an old house is like searching for an HMO that's willing to take on an old man as a patient. There's a well-founded fear of unexpected ailments that can run up the cost of treatment of the elderly man. He may appear to be in great health for his age, but a routine checkup is liable to turn up heart disease or cancer or some other condition that's much more expensive to treat than the premiums the patient pays will ever cover. The real profit in medicine comes from treating the healthy. It's the same when it comes to renovating houses. Once the price is set, the less work that's needed, the more money the contractor makes.

It was no wonder, then, that few contractors would even talk to me about renovating the house once I described its age and condition. One contractor cut me off before I got halfway through my list of repairs. "Telling me what you want done is meaningless," he said. "Once you start opening up walls, there's no telling what you're going to find. For me to make it worth my time, you're probably looking at twenty thousand dollars up front with you covering all costs, plus a percentage."

That wasn't the kind of arrangement I was looking for. I was willing to pay a fair price, pay what the work was worth. But I didn't want to give a contractor incentives to take shortcuts in labor and scrimp on supplies or, on the other hand, to draw things out and buy materials for big markups in order to make the margin of profit as large as possible. I thought about Mr. Mashburn or Mathews or whoever the man was whose name I found inside the wall. What kind of agreement did he have with my grandfather almost sixty years ago? It would have been a buyer's market back then, during the Depression. I'm sure a house builder was grateful to get the job. He probably had two incentives driving him: first, get the job done quickly, because the sooner it was finished, the sooner he got paid; and second, do the job well, because his name was going to be on it.

It definitely wasn't a buyer's market when I went looking for a contractor. A couple I found in the Jackson phone book were too busy to take on more work or were no longer doing renovations, concentrating on new construction instead. The first contractor I got to come out gave the house a cursory inspection. When he spoke, however, his tone was grave, as if he knew the house's deepest and most malevolent secrets. "You're going to have to jack the house up to fix the foundation," he said. "I wouldn't want to be around when you do it. An old, two-story house like that? The whole place could come down on you at any time. You might be able to find somebody who's willing to do it. It's going to cost you, though. You'd be better off building from scratch."

The second contractor to come out had a completely different outlook. "Jacking the house up is no big deal," he said. "We do it all the time. It'll be easy. No big deal."

He promised to write up an estimate. But he showed where his interest lay as he was about to leave. "You know, I could probably build you a new house for less than you'll have to pay to renovate," he said.

"I know. That's a possibility, but I'd like to save the house if I can. Why don't you give me an estimate for a new house as well as for the repairs I mentioned?"

"Sure, I can do that," he said. "How many acres you got out here?"

"A little less than five or so."

"That's enough to subdivide," he said. "You do that and you could make enough to pay for your house and make a profit, too."

"Well, I haven't given any thought to subdividing. That really isn't what I had in mind. If I like your estimate, when would you be able to start work?"

"We're pretty busy right now. I think you'll find pretty much everybody is. There's a lot of building going on around here. I expect we'd be about ready to get to this work sometime around October."

It was late spring. The contractor was telling me it would be fall before he would have time to drive the first nail at the house. That was too long to wait, it seemed to me. Maybe I was showing that lack of patience Dan Curl warned me about, but I was thinking that first contractor had it right. If I didn't go ahead and get it fixed, the place would probably fall down on top of me.

+>= =<+

While looking for a contractor to work on the house, I got started reclaiming the land—which meant vanquishing two foes, kudzu and fire ants. If the legal rule that possession is nine-tenths of the law also applies to nature, then kudzu and fire ants—both ubiquitous—were the true claimants of the farmland. Taken together they easily covered 90 percent of the acreage.

Kudzu is the vine that ate the South. It was imported from Japan in the early 1900s as an ornamental plant and eventually was used to fight erosion and feed cattle. The plant was spectacularly successful as ground cover, and it did a fine job of keeping the soil from being washed away by the rain. Of course, it would have kept the soil from being washed away by oceans too, so thoroughly did its extensive root system hold the dirt together. Kudzu's career as cattle feed faded, however, even though farmers said their cows loved it. I suspect cows lost their taste for kudzu, just as a child might lose his taste for chocolate ice cream if he woke up every morning to find an infinite serving of it spread out as far as the eye can see.

Kudzu lore took root in the South. Poet James Dickey wrote about people waking up to find their windows tinged green by the plant as it inexorably pressed in on them. There's an old joke about a city slicker who moves out to the country. He wants to say something nice when he visits the farmer next door. He looks at the kudzu covering one of the farmer's fields and says, "My, that's a fine crop you got there. How do you get it to grow?" The farmer goes over to the vine and pinches off a small piece. "Well, son," he says, "you take this over to your place, drop it on the ground and run like hell."

Anyone who has driven Southern back roads knows there is truth in even the most farfetched stories about how fast kudzu grows. There are places where it covers the land mile after mile. It shrouds telephone poles, trees, and entire abandoned houses. And do the eyes play tricks, or are those the shapes of people and animals draped in green?

According to Gary L. Wade of the Georgia Extension Service, the Civilian Conservation Corps began planting kudzu for erosion control in the 1940s. By the middle of the decade, more than five hundred thousand acres of Southern soil were covered by kudzu. But the rapacious vine wasn't satisfied with that small portion. It spread rapidly from its designated plots. Wade says the vine grew so fast that it even covered railroad tracks in some areas, making them slippery and dangerous for trains. By 1960, Wade says, the plant that was supposed to save the South had become its sworn enemy. Kudzu turned out to be the region's most destructive invader since Sherman made his march to the sea.

I don't think an inch of kudzu ever took root on the land while my grandfather worked it. Now, it must cover four of the five acres that are left. In the back there's a tree that's at least forty feet tall, every inch of it covered in kudzu. Somewhere back there is the creek where I used to catch sunfish and turtles. You would have an easier time hacking your way through the rain forest to reach the Amazon than getting to that creek through the kudzu vines.

When I wrote a newspaper column about my declared war on kudzu, I wasn't surprised when readers responded with advice on how to get rid of the vine (douse it with the most potent herbicide allowed by law; bulldoze it and burn it; put goats on the land and let them chew it down to the roots). However, I was surprised to hear from a bunch of people extolling the plant's virtues. It's great in salads, said one reader. The Japanese use starch from kudzu's roots—which are tubers like sweet potatoes and can weight up to a hundred pounds—to make tofu and as a thickener in other dishes. The tough vine can be woven into baskets or used to make paper. And kudzu has several medicinal uses, said yet another reader.

I told a friend I hadn't realized I was sitting on such a valuable crop. "If kudzu salad, kudzu tofu, or kudzu medicine ever catches on," I said, "I'll be in the money."

Meanwhile, I bought a machete and kept it sharpened.

+>— —<+

Fire ants are accidental tourists who overstayed their welcome. Unlike the defenders of kudzu, no fire ant apologists wrote to accuse me of unfairly maligning the insect. I'm not surprised. Even though a southern band and a professional football team took its name, this is a pest no one can love.

The first fire ants probably arrived in the U.S. at the port city of Mobile, Alabama, as South American stowaways on cargo ships. They may have been inadvertently loaded in soil used as ballast for the ships. The Southern states had the heat and moisture of the ants' native habitat. And the insects' natural predators were absent. That combination allowed fire ants to thrive and spread rapidly across the South.

Experts date the United States' first infestation of fire ants somewhere between the early 1920s and the early 1940s. One account places their arrival right at 1940, the year my grandparents' house was built. They were first reported in Georgia in the early 1950s. As the fire ants' range grew, so did their legend. There are stories of fire ant mounds so high that tractors flipped over trying to climb them in the fields. Farmers were said to find cows killed and stripped to the bone overnight. And unfortunate household pets supposedly were sucked whole down ant holes, like cartoon characters pulled through a keyhole.

Forget exaggeration. What fire ants actually do is bad enough. First, they muscle out all other ants; then, once they've established themselves, they colonize like crazy. Their closely crowded mounds look like a rash upon the ground. As spring broke and the ground thawed in the months after we bought the farm, I noticed the little bumps of earth everywhere during my drives down to Jackson. The subsoil they bring up has an eerie incandescence, a color that glows in comparison to the red clay on the surface. It makes me wonder if this, and not their burning sting, explains the "fire" in the ants' name.

At first, the extent of the ants' presence on the farm wasn't evident. But as I began clearing the land and cutting back the overgrowth, I saw that they were everywhere. Their mounds—each a few inches high—were revealed when the tall grass and the weeds were gone. A fire ant mound is transformed if it is disturbed in any way. The ants come out so quickly and in such numbers that it appears the dirt has come to life. And the ants are very aggressive. Once agitated, they'll deliver their painful bite to anything they crawl onto.

There are, of course, entire books written about these insects and their behavior. But everything I need to know about fire ants I learned before I was in kindergarten. I'm sure of this because of another of my vivid memories of the farm. I was playing in a plowed but unplanted field. I didn't see the ant mound until I stepped on it with a bare foot. The ants began biting immediately. It didn't take them long to climb up my leg and reach every part of my body.

I ran screaming to Grandma. She filled a washtub with well water and put me in it. I remember the ants as they were washed from my body—hundreds of them, it seemed, the dead ones floating on the surface, the ones still alive walking on the water. But, most of all, I remember the pain of the ant bites and the welts they left all over my body.

I grew up believing Grandma had magical powers, but only because she could and did perform magic. Like most women who lived out in the country, she was a shaman. People didn't go to see a doctor unless it involved a broken bone or a life-or-death crisis. Prescription medicines were expensive. Having home remedies and treatments for the everyday ailments and injuries of farm life was essential.

Grandma was our medicine woman. She took dipping snuff from between her cheek and gum and dabbed it on wasp or bee stings to make the pain go away. She bandaged a piece of fatback and a "silver" coin—a new dime or half-dollar worked best—to a deep splinter wound to draw the wood out. She washed away ring worm and other skin conditions with a woman's urine. She put butter on minor burns. Serious burns required the intervention of a spiritual healer, preferably a woman who had been given the gift of healing to compensate for never having seen her father or heard his voice (such cases were much more rare back then, of course).

My grandmother's medicines met the same standard the most sophisticated drugs must meet today: They relieved people's suffering while doing no harm. They worked because Grandma believed they worked and convinced her patients that they worked. I don't remember exactly what magic she performed after the ants had been washed away and I stepped from the washtub covered in ant bites. Perhaps it was dabs of snuff. Whatever it was, I'm sure it worked. It worked because Grandma prepped her patient by saying, "Let me put this on you, baby. It'll make you feel all better."

My revenge for that first encounter with fire ants was a long time coming, but it finally began when I became owner of the land they had occupied for some forty years. I went to a hardware store and bought ant poison. It promised the ant colony would be wiped out within three days of sprinkling two tablespoons around the mound. "Kills the entire nest, including the queen," the label

promised. I sprinkled the white powder with some skepticism.
This seemed too easy. The tenacity of fire ants is legendary.
Getting rid of them couldn't be this simple. But it worked. Three
days later I found the ant hills I had treated as dead as western
ghost towns. No ants poured out when I poked the dirt with a
stick. There was no movement at all. The only ants in sight were
dead, their tiny bodies bloated, like flood-killed cattle found in
the fields after the water recedes.

⊬═ ═⊬

The print was small, but the words in the newspaper ad jumped
out at me. "Foundations repaired, floors leveled," it read.
"Commercial and residential. No job too large, no job too
small."

I was scanning the classified section of the *Atlanta Constitution*
after deciding no one in Jackson had both the time and the talent
to do the foundation work on the house. I hoped to find a contractor in Atlanta willing to make the 45-minute trip to the farm.
That was how I found Superior Structures and Jim Gann.

The answering service picked up when I dialed the number.
The operator said she would give Jim Gann my message. My
telephone rang less than five minutes later. "Mr. Head, this is Jim
Gann," he said. "I understand you got some work for me."

Jim's voice was deep, and so was his Southern drawl. I
explained the work I wanted done on the farmhouse and asked if
he took jobs as far away as Butts County.

"Going down there is no problem at all," he said. "We can get
a motel or drive down every day. We'd probably take a motel so
we can get everything done for you as soon as possible."

I asked when he could take a look and give me an estimate.
"You tell me when it's convenient for you," he said.

"I can drive down first thing in the morning," I said. "If you
can meet me somewhere we can go together."

"How 'bout we meet at the Kentucky Fried Chicken across

from the stadium?" he said. "Would eight o'clock be too early for you? We can jump on I-75 and shoot right down there."

The KFC parking lot was empty when I got there a little before eight the next morning. Several cars had pulled in by eight-thirty, but none of them were Jim Gann's. I worried that I might be in the wrong place. Was there another Kentucky Fried Chicken in the neighborhood? Jim said the one across from the stadium. But did he mean Turner Field—the new stadium—or Atlanta-Fulton County—the old stadium that was no longer in use? I would give it a few more minutes before scouting the area for an alternate KFC.

About fifteen minutes later an old van, its rear end sagging, limped into the parking lot. Two men got out. One was a tall, heavyset, barrel-chested man; the other was shorter and slightly built. They walked toward the truck, where I sat waiting.

"Mr. Head?" I nodded and opened the door to get out. "Jim Gann," the man continued, extending his hand. "This is my brother Gene. I apologize for being late. I got a tile man was supposed to meet me this morning at a job we promised to get finished today. When he didn't show I had to go get him. Let's go ahead and get rollin'. You mind we go in your truck if you got room for the three of us?"

"There's a jump seat in the cab," I said. "It might be a little tight."

"Oh, that'll be fine," Jim Gann said. "Gene has rid in worse."

Jim had a beefy, red, open face. What hair he had he let grow long so he could comb it around to cover his bald pate. He was as outgoing as he looked. His brother had a closed countenance and was quiet. He sat behind us and spoke only when prompted by Jim.

"Remember that time when I came and got you down in Florida and brung you back to help me with that big job?" Jim would say.

"Yeah, I remember," Gene would answer. "I was livin' the life down there. Fishin' all day and drinkin' beer all night. But I come up and helped you, didn't I?"

Jim did most of the talking. Mostly he spoke of the old houses
he had worked on. He and Gene jacked a historic house in
Decatur off its foundation so it could be moved to make way for
rapid rail construction. They did foundation repair on a house
built before the Civil War. "Would you believe it? There wasn't
a single nail in it," he said. "It was put together entire with wood
pegs." And they had worked on houses all over—lots of them farther away than Jackson.

By the time we reached the farm Jim's tales of the houses he
rescued from demolition had just about convinced me he was the
contractor I was looking for.

"Let's get under there and have a look at her," Jim said as soon
as we were out of the truck. I put on my coveralls. Jim and Gene
went as they were.

"Good Lord-o-Mercy!" Jim shook his head as he inspected the
repair work at the back of the house beneath the kitchen and
bathroom. "They didn't do a bit of good here. Look at this joist
they put in. It ain't doing a thing but hangin' there. Not sup-
porting nothing."

Other added braces and beams drew similar condemnation.
"Whoever did this didn't have no idea what they was doin'," Jim
said.

We inched toward the front of the house. The crawl space got
tighter as we made our way. I was concerned about Jim's bulk. I
imagined him getting wedged in and my having to call the fire
department to get him out. "There's not much room up there,"
I said.

"This here is roomy," Jim said. "We worked in much closer
quarters than this, ain't we, Gene?"

"You got that right," Gene said.

Jim's flashlight beam played across the foundation at the front
of the house.

"Well, they don't build houses like they used to," he said, "and
sometimes you just have to say thank God for that. Those old-
time carpenters, bless their hearts. Back then they just had to do
the best they could with what they had.

"Look at that," he went on. "They mixed and matched to get this sill to run all the way across and come out even. They got two-by-sixes, two-by-tens and—I can't tell what that is—nailed together. It can't be stable. We goin' to have to jack it up and pull 'em out—put something new in all the way across."

"Two-by-tens ought to do it," Gene said. "You could splice 'em and face 'em with three-quarter-inch plywood to help brace 'em." It was the first thing I had heard him say without being spoken to.

"Yeah, that'd work," Jim said. "That'd be plenty strong enough to carry the load."

We made the circuit inspecting the foundation. Jim pointed out wood sound enough to keep and wood so damaged by insects or rot that it had to be replaced. The inventory showed most of the foundation needed replacement.

The estimate Jim Gann scribbled on a proposed contract promised to repair the foundation, replacing damaged wood where necessary. In addition, new footing would be poured and concrete blocks laid for the sill to rest on at the back of the house. Floors would be made level. The contractor would be responsible for obtaining work permits and for complying with local building codes. The work would be completed in a week to ten days. All of this would be done for just under ten thousand dollars.

Ten thousand dollars didn't sound like much compared to what other contractors had told me. But it probably was several times what my grandfather paid for the house. And this was just the first step in the restoration. Still, Jim Gann made it sound like a bargain.

"I don't believe you'll find anybody can come close to that price," he said. "And I know ain't *nobody* going to match the quality of our work. When we get done, the foundation will be better'n when it was brand new, I guarantee."

We were standing in the driveway getting ready to load into the truck for the drive back to Atlanta. "I'd like to do what I can to save the house," I said. "Several people have told me I should just tear it down and build a new one."

"Tear down this nice old house?" Jim said. He sounded truly incredulous. "My goodness, no! There's no reason at all to do that, is there, Gene?"

"No reason," Gene said. "Lots of good wood left in that house."

"What you plannin' to do with it, Mr. Head?" Jim asked. "You goin' to sell it?"

"No. It was my grandparents' house. I bought it to keep it in the family. I'm going to restore it and have it as a place everyone can come visit, some place for the family to gather on special occasions."

"My, my. Ain't that a wonderful thing to do?" Jim said. "I wish more people had that kind of respect for their family and for old houses. That's a mighty good thing you're doin'."

This was, no doubt, part of the sales pitch. But Jim Gann had that knack the best salesmen have. Even as you knew he was selling, he made you want to be sold, because before he sold you, he sold himself into believing in what he was selling.

When I told other people about my dream for the farm, they tried ever so gently to shake me awake before it was too late. Jim, on the other hand, got misty-eyed himself and said, "What a wonderful dream." And he sounded as if it came from the heart.

I was sold.

CHAPTER 4

My grandparents left their imprints everywhere on the farmhouse and the land. At the turn of every corner I conjure a memory of them, a virtual holographic image. Their handiwork is mostly in ruins now, victims of years of neglect and abuse. But what remains makes me think of them and remember them as if they were still here, though my grandmother is almost a decade dead, and my grandfather three.

I fear trying to give a detailed description of what they were like, because I'm not sure I ever really knew them. Some things I remember about them do stand out. I can't recall a cross word between them, except when Grandpa was on one of his weekend "drunks." Grandma took the keys to the truck and hid them, all the while fussing at him about drinking and driving. "You're going to kill yourself or somebody else," she would say. Grandpa flopped drunkenly down into his favorite chair in the living room and demanded his keys. "That's my truck!" he said. "I can drive it any time I wanna drive it." Even those fights ended peacefully. Once my grandfather sat in his chair or lay down on the bed, he didn't get up. He sank into a deep, snoring sleep. If he made it to the bed, Grandma pulled his shoes off and tucked him in like a child.

He called her Lady. She called him Poppa. When he was in the fields and she called him in to dinner or supper, those names echoed back from the hill to the west where the sun went to hide at the end of the day. Grandma would call out first: "Paaaaaapaaaa!" "Hey, Lady!" Grandpa yelled back, and they kept it up until each was sure the other had heard. Their voices bounced off the hill, intermingling with the echoes until it seemed the names themselves were calling to each other.

If I can't remember my grandparents ever cross at each other, I also can't recall a display of affection between them. Of course, my grandmother got out of bed before sunup to fix breakfast for my grandfather and spent most of the day doing housework to make his life more comfortable. My grandfather trudged to the fields at first light and spent most of the day growing crops or earning money for the things that made my grandmother's life as comfortable as possible. I'm not counting those as displays of affection, though they surely were. I'm talking about the small things: a hug, a kiss, the holding of hands. I never saw any of that.

They were more than thirty years into their marriage by the time I was old enough to take note of such things. Were they prone to public displays of affection when they were young, only to put that behavior aside as childish as the years passed? Probably not, given the time and place in which they grew up. I wish I could have known them when they were young. Seeing who they once were would help me understand the people they became.

I had never seen a photograph of my grandparents when they were young until an aunt came across one and brought copies to a family reunion. The picture was taken in the front yard of the farmhouse, underneath the big tree that still stands. Grandma looks directly at the camera. She looks resolute, like the kind of woman who very well could tell her husband that she was packing up and taking the children back to Georgia, no matter what he planned to do. She stands beside Grandpa, who is seated. Her left arm reaches from behind him, her hand resting lightly on his left shoulder. My grandfather, wearing suspenders and a dress shirt open at the collar, does not look at the camera. He squints toward the west. His mouth is set in an almost-frown. He looks like a man assessing his land as the sun sets behind it, a man who decides he did not do enough during the day just done, and who knows he must rise with the sun the next day and work harder.

A camera does not capture people's souls, much less reveal them. But that one photograph is all I have to supplement what I know about my grandparents from the days when they already were old. I will take what meager insight I might glean from the picture and combine it with those memories and ghosts evoked by the farm. I will accept scraps from any source as I try to piece together a portrait of the man and woman who molded the house and the land as a sculptor would shape her work. Of course, I was like clay in their hands during the many childhood days I spent on the farm, and they left their imprints on me, too.

+>==< >==<+

I see now that my grandmother was a genuine aesthete, though I did not know that word as a child and wouldn't have applied it to her if I had. Her love for beauty was unpretentious and practical. It was so elemental, so much a part of her nature, that an undiscerning observer would not have picked it out from her day-to-day routine. Grandma herself would never use such a fancy word as "artwork" to describe the beauty she created or collected. To her, it was simply a part of housework and yard work.

She made quilts from rags, the waste from other sewing projects, or cloth worn out in its first incarnation. These swaths were sewn or tied into patterns of colors and shapes that pleased the eye and occupied the subconscious in a game of decoding. Grandma appreciated the beauty of well-made quilts, but to her they were mainly to keep us warm on cold winter nights.

She used delicate threads to weave lace doilies more intricate and beautiful than any spider's web. To Grandma, they helped protect upholstery from the grime of constant human contact.

She stitched gossamer cloth with invisible thread, creating

curtains that floated and undulated in the slow-moving summer air. To my grandmother, they simply provided a little privacy and faint relief from the sun's heating rays.

And just as nature abhors a vacuum, my grandmother hated empty spaces in her house. She collected objects to fill bare corners and shelves—a large shell that shared the sound of the sea with any child who knew to listen; a small ball of crystal glass; china figurines of people and animals; starfish; polished stones that felt heavy in my palm; plates engraved with scenes of a country life of privilege and leisure my grandmother could only dream of.

My grandmother's most beautiful works of art were the flowers and other flora she planted in abundance around the farmhouse. If you complimented her on that beauty, she would say it was God's creation, not her handiwork. Yet she chose the plants, decided on their placement, and gave them the care they needed to flourish. She had a genius and love for coaxing nature's lovely gifts from the ground. My grandmother could even make dirt itself look pretty— literally. Like most women out in the country, the idea of a lawn never occurred to her. In fact, she was ever vigilant against the encroachment of grass into her yards. Any blade showing its face was immediately attacked with a hoe. The yards had to be bare dirt, and that dirt had to be swept periodically. In doing that sweeping, Grand na, like so many women back then, turned the ground into a canvas. She bundled long twigs and tied them together to fashion homemade yard brooms. When she swept, each of the twigs scratched a line in the dirt. My grandmother used sweeping motions that laid down these lines into swirling circles and semi-circles, and parallel lines. The result was a mosaic of interlocking geometric shapes. Like mandalas, the sand painting of Buddhist monks, the artwork lasted barely as long as it took the artist to create it. But, then, that must have been the point. Grandma never explained why she put so much effort into that yard-sweeping. I like to think she felt that to create a transitory object of beauty is to create true beauty, something that in this world does not last and can never be owned.

+⇒ ⇒+

Those artistic talents my grandmother did not pass down to me. I don't have her knack with knickknacks. My efforts at collecting quickly turn to clutter. I'm better off being a minimalist, keeping bare those empty spaces Grandma filled with simple, beautiful objects.

Her passion for plants passed me by, too. I am plant dumb. When I picked up the sling blade and began the job of reclaiming the front yard, every plant was at risk, whether wicked weed or friendly flower. I usually can't tell the difference. Of course, someone who doesn't even know the names of plants has no business trying to grow them.

But my grandmother loved to read, and she loved to hear or tell stories. Those passions did rub off on me, and that, as much as anything else, was why I first turned to writing. She read anything she could get her hands on whenever she had a few minutes or more to spare. She read the Bible not just because she believed it to be the word of God—and that she fervently believed—but also because it was full of good stories. True confession magazines with their "women's stories" were favorites. She read *Ebony* and *Jet* magazines, along with *Life* and *National Geographic*. Anything she finished reading and put down, I picked up at the first opportunity.

And my grandmother told me stories. These were never the bedtime variety, with animals who talked and taught life's little lessons. They were stories about real people. All were true, or, at the very least, could have been true. Grandma was liable to tell a story any time she sat down, either because she had to sit while doing a chore like shelling peas or churning butter, or because she had the time to sit at the end of the day or when a friend dropped by to swap stories. Those leisure-time tales were told on the front porch. Storytelling, when done well, has a rhythm to it. The rocking chair my grandmother sat in on the front porch was the metronome to her stories. Her rocks were short and quick when the story had action and excitement. They were long and leisurely when the story was a gentle rumination.

Grandma told me of the first time Grandpa came courting. They had never met, but he had seen her and asked her father's permission to come visit. She stood at a window with one of her sisters as he arrived wearing his best clothes and riding in a wagon hitched to a mule.

"Here comes Buddy Fitch to court you," her sister teased.

She looked out as he got down from the wagon. Then she gave her first assessment of the young man with whom she would spend the next half-century.

"Why," she said, "he ain't nothing but a boy."

She told me fantastic tales of fish falling from the sky, of manatees grazing on water lilies, of oranges growing in the front yard.

She told me about the time a hailstorm came up during Sunday service. The preacher urged everyone to stay calm. "God will protect us," he said. But the storm intensified and the chunks of falling ice grew larger, until it seemed they would batter their way through the tin roof. The preacher panicked and fled from the church to a grove of pine trees. He wrapped his arms around the trunk of the biggest one and held on tight. He might have been killed if two deacons had not gone out and pried him from the tree and brought him back inside the church.

"Now wasn't that something?" Grandma said at the end of the story. "There he was, a man of God who got so scared he ran out of God's house into a hailstorm. Even the Lord can't protect you if you act that foolish."

And she told me stories her grandfather told her, stories about the days of slavery and the Civil War, about the mistress saying the Yankees were coming and the slaves having to bury the silverware and take the livestock to hide in the woods until the Yankees were gone.

Grandma's stories, her flowers, her eclectic collection of space-fillers, made the farm a place of wonder and excitement and pleasure for me. She made the farm the place I could go back to, as that Jackson Browne song says, to "see where my beginnings had gone."

Memories of my grandfather are not as sweet. How could they be? They come to me mostly while I'm working on the farm. When I look at the fields now overgrown with waist-high grass, weeds, and brambles, I see him plowing behind his mule. I haul neatly bagged trash to the county dumpster, and I see him driving his beat-up pickup loaded down with garbage people paid him a few dollars to take to the dump. Stacking bricks I find scattered around the back yard, I see him rummaging through the rubble of a demolished building for bricks he had been told he could have, and which, after chipping the mortar from them, he would sell for a penny each.

As I said before, he was a man who did not wait for work to find him. He hunted it down and attacked it. No sooner had he finished with what had to be done on the farm than he was off doing odd jobs somewhere else. I admire him for shouldering his responsibilities and working so hard to provide for his family. But I also believe there were times when his work became a mania for him, or perhaps as much of an escape as his drinking was. And he could not see beyond back-breaking work as the way to make it in this world.

My mother told me about the superintendent of schools coming by the farm to talk to Grandpa about allowing her to come out of school early and go down to the college in Fort Valley. "She's smart enough to get a scholarship right now," the man said. "She can study to be a teacher, and we need more colored teachers."

Grandpa looked away as he answered. "I can't do it," he said. "I need her to stay here and help with the work."

"But Buddy, everything will be paid for. It won't cost you anything."

My grandfather spoke firmly—probably as firmly as he dared speak to a white man. "No suh. Like I said. She got to stay here and work."

I can remember seeing Grandpa do something for the sheer fun of it only once. Even my fondest memories of him have to do with work. He tried to teach me to plow once, telling me to call out "Gee!" if I wanted the mule to turn right (or was it left?) and "Haw" if I wanted it to turn left (or was it right?). I loved to sit up front beside him in the wagon as the mule pulled it slowly up the country road into town to pick up a load of feed or some other supplies that I would help load.

But there were plenty of jobs that were no fun at all—like gathering and selling firewood. We went to a site where pulp-wooders had clear-cut a stand of pine trees. Grandpa and I loaded the best of their leavings into his truck. Then we drove to a place where there was a gas-powered saw with a huge blade. Grandpa fed the wood to the saw, cutting it into firewood length. I would pick it up and toss it into the truck. By the time the cutting was done we were covered with sawdust and I carried a vision of that saw blade flying free and cutting me in half.

Once, a feed store owner offered to let him have the spillage from his grain conveyor just to have the area around the machine cleaned. My grandfather and I went down into the dark bowels of the silo—a small and hot space with a thick layer of grain covering the floor. Grandpa scooped it up with a shovel and fed it into burlap bags I held open. The already-stifling air soon was filled with dust stirred up from the grain. The handkerchiefs we tied around our faces were little help. Relief came only when we took filled bags and put them into the truck. Grandpa used these brief breaks in the fresh air to roll himself a cigarette. He had large, thick-veined hands strengthened and hardened by work. Yet they were nimble enough to tap tobacco onto a small rectangle of delicate, tissue-thin paper and roll it into a cylinder without a tear. He sealed the cigarette by running his tongue along the paper's trailing edge before pressing it gently down.

We went back down into the choking dust and heat after Grandpa finished his smoke. I didn't realize how closely we had courted disaster until years later when I read about grain elevator explosions caused by a spark igniting the highly combustible dust.

I joined my grandfather in lots of dangerous jobs, but I was never seriously hurt doing any of them. In fact, the most pain I ever felt working with him was not physical. It was a Saturday, and two of my brothers and I were helping him on his garbage route. We went from house to house picking up trash cans—most of them converted fifty-five-gallon drums—and emptying them into the back of the pickup truck. Two of us kids had to ride in the truck bed with the trash. The truck was soon loaded with all kinds of garbage—paper, plastic containers, broken toys, spoiled food, ashes left from trash-burning.

By early evening we were almost done. We were taking a load to the dump when Grandpa drove slowly past a yard where a large group of boys played basketball. I sat in the back of the truck with one of my brothers. We were covered from head to toe with filth, barely distinguishable from the pile of garbage. Someone pointed at us. The game stopped. Among those staring were kids who were my classmates and friends. Someone shouted something—I couldn't understand what they said—and everyone laughed. My face burned with a shame whose heat seared something deep inside me. If I had seen that moment coming and been given time to burrow into the garbage before my friends saw me, I would have done it. I thought I would never survive that humiliation.

Of course, I did survive—lived and learned from it, in fact. I learned a lesson that, looking back now, I can see my grandfather taught me over and over again. He was a man who shouldered responsibility for most of his life. He insisted on doing so without owing anyone anything. He showed that there is dignity in even the most demeaning work.

+⇒ ⇐+

One summer day, as the setting sun sucked the heat from the air and favored us with a rare cool evening, two of my brothers and I played baseball in the farmhouse driveway. Jimmy was pitching, Fred was at bat, and I was the catcher. We paid little notice when Grandpa turned his pickup into the drive and parked behind us.

He had been working at something, as usual. His overalls were dirty and his gait had a weariness as he walked toward the house. But, for some reason, he stopped and watched us. We went on playing. Down low in my catcher's squat, I put my right hand between my legs and put down two fingers, signaling Jimmy that I wanted him to throw a curve ball. My glove was the target on the outside edge of the piece of wood that passed for home plate, away from Fred in the left-handed batter's box. Jimmy went into his windup and let the ball fly on a straight line off the plate until it made a small arch and caught the outside corner. "Strike!" I called.

Before Fred could argue, Grandpa asked, "What kind of pitch was that?"

"That was a curve ball," I said.

"When I played, we called that a out-shoot," he said. "Let me show you how I used to pitch."

He walked over to Jimmy, who handed him the ball the way a manager would give it to a relief pitcher. The ball wasn't simply flipped to him; it was handed over almost grudgingly, as if to say, "I am entrusting the game to you. Don't show me my faith is misplaced."

Grandpa looked at me. "This is a out-shoot," he said. He went into an elaborate windup, pumping his arms several times before rocking back and throwing. The ball came in harder than I expected, but there was little movement on it. Not much of a curve, I thought. He motioned for me to throw the ball back to him, though he had not borrowed Jimmy's glove. I lobbed it back, and he grabbed it out of the air with bare hands.

"This is a in-shoot," he said. Again, the long windup. The pitch wasn't as hard this time, but it actually did break away from the left-handed batter's box. I knew what a screwball was, but I had never seen anyone actually throw one until that moment.

"This is a drop," Grandpa said when he had the ball again. This was the hardest pitch yet, and it did dive down like a sinker ball. I was impressed, and Grandpa had a satisfied look on his face.

"Let me have a knock," he said, walking to Fred and taking the bat from him.

I knew then that Grandpa had been too much impressed with
his pitching prowess and was about to embarrass himself.
Throwing a baseball is one thing, but hitting one is quite another.
It's the most difficult skill to master in sports. Grandpa was in his
mid-sixties. Old eyes, slow reflexes. He would have no chance, I
thought. When he took his stance at the plate, I felt sorry for him.
He stood straight up, with no crouch at all, in the right-handed
batter's box. The bat was held with his hands slightly apart, like
the grip Ty Cobb used. There wasn't much power in that grip.

Jimmy wound up and threw the ball toward the plate. It was
up in the strike zone, above the belt. I reached to catch it, certain
Grandpa would either let it pass or swing and miss. He swung,
but he did not miss. There was a satisfying "Smack!" as the
wooden bat met the leather-covered ball. I looked up and saw the
ball climbing into the sky. It grew smaller and smaller, seeming to
travel forever. The baseball went beyond the driveway into the
back yard, beyond the shed and the outhouse and into some
bushes. I stood there amazed, while Grandpa admired his shot.
He didn't say anything. Just handed the bat back to Fred and
walked slowly into the house.

The child I was back then thought he had witnessed a man-
sized feat. The ball must have carried far enough to clear the fence
in any major league ballpark, I thought. But I can walk off the
distance now. The flight of the ball actually was around 250 feet.
That's not all that far by baseball standards. Back then, though, it
really was halfway to forever. It was something to see.

That was the one and only time I ever saw my grandfather at
play. That made it memorable for me. It must have been memorable for him, too. He must have seen something more than the
long arc of the ball as he stood there at home plate admiring his
hit. He must have seen the boy he once was, a boy who could
throw an in-shoot, an out-shoot, and a drop, and who could hit
'em like Ty Cobb used to. He must have seen a boy who enjoyed
having a good time, a boy everyone called "Buddy."

CHAPTER 5

If Job were around today, the Good Lord would not test his faith and patience with the torments described in the Bible. He wouldn't use fire from heaven to burn Job's sheep and his servants. He wouldn't send marauding hordes to steal Job's livestock and kill even more servants. He wouldn't send the whirlwind to blow down the house, killing Job's sons and daughters. No, the test God would put Job through today would be much more torturous than those standard tribulations. God would make Job a homeowner, and He would put him at the mercy of contractors.

One thing that makes dealing with unreliable contractors such an exquisite torment is that you have to pay the contractor for torturing you. But it's not just the money. It's also what was supposed to break Job, though on a smaller scale. It is the feeling of being let down by someone you trust and in whom you've invested your faith.

I had been pleased with the work Jim Gann did on the foundation. The job took longer than he promised, but that was no major problem. When one of the subcontractors failed to do his work, Jim stepped in and made sure it got done. My initial faith in him had been justified. So I didn't hesitate when he asked to make bids on the next phase of the renovation—rewiring and replumbing.

We agreed to meet early on a Tuesday morning at a fast-food restaurant that was on my way down to the farm. Jim was already there when I arrived. That was a good sign, I thought. Ever the salesman, he began making his pitch as soon as I walked through the door.

"I got your plumber and your electrician right here," he said. "You give me the word and I can send 'em down there this morning. They're ready to get goin'. They'll work all day and take a motel room down there so they can get right back at it first thing in the mornin'. I figure they'll be done four days after you let 'em get started. We're going to let each of 'em tell you what they're goin' to do and all you got to do is give us the word."

Jim looked across the restaurant to a booth where three men sat hunched over their breakfasts of biscuit sandwiches and coffee. "Austin!" Jim Gann's voice boomed. "Come on over here, old man, and tell Mr. Head what you gonna do for him."

The man who walked toward us was short and muscular. He had the broad shoulders and outsized forearms of someone whose work involves heavy lifting. Jim Gann put his hand on the man's shoulder. "Austin, this is John Head. John, this here is Austin. He's as old as dirt and been working on houses all his life. Austin's done a ton of work for me and I can guarantee you he's a first-class plumber."

Austin's handshake was as firm as expected. "Pleased to meet you, Mr. John Head," he said. His voice had the unmistakable lilt of the Caribbean. He sat down across the table from me and told me what he was going to do for me, which, he said repeatedly, was anything I wanted.

"We gonna do everything perfect for you," he said. "If we don't do everything the way you want it, we'll do it over again."

Jim stepped in to get down to specifics. The work would follow the floor plan I had given him. The new plumbing included the addition of a bathroom upstairs, a corner shower stall in the downstairs bathroom, and connections for a washing machine.

New copper pipe would be laid from the water meter, a spigot added in the back, and other improvements made to bring the house up to code. Austin simply nodded as Jim reeled off the details.

Jim dispatched Austin once he was done. "Tell Ted to come on over here," he said.

"John, this is the electrician, Ted Watkins," Jim said. "Ted, this is John Head."

"Nice to meet you," Ted said as he shook my hand. He was very tall, and not thin. He seemed nervous, and he looked away a lot as he talked. Ted opened a small notebook. He had a long list of specifications for the improvements he would make at the house. All work would meet local code requirements. Wiring for telephones and cable TV would be included. So would connections for smoke detectors. Ted went through other details. Jim Gann fidgeted.

Ted also had a list of questions for me. "Are these sketches drawn to scale?" he said. He asked about placement of outlets, light fixtures, and switches. "Are you definitely going to have an entertainment center here?" he asked, pointing to a bedroom corner on the first-floor layout.

Jim Gann interrupted. "All John wants to know right now is that you'll do a good job of rewiring the house and that all the work will be up to code," he said. "You can get down to plugs and lights later."

Ted seemed deflated as he closed his notebook and walked back to his table.

"Here are the numbers they came up with for the work," Jim said, handing me a piece of paper. "This'll be in the contract. It won't cost you any more than this. You ready to get 'em started this morning?"

The total on the paper came to nine thousand dollars. That was less than another contractor bid for the plumbing work alone. Jim had been low man on the foundation work, too, and he came through. I made up my mind right then and there to give him the work, but I didn't want to tell him that immediately. It would be better to give the impression that I'm thinking carefully about all of this and not being driven by his sales pitch, I thought.

"Let me think about it and call you this afternoon or tonight," I said.

"That means a day wasted," Jim said. "They're all available right now. They ain't got nothing else going, but that don't mean another job might not come up. I'd hate to have to tell you that you gotta wait."

"I know," I said. "I just want to give it some thought. What if I decided to go ahead with the plumbing and wait on the electrical?" I asked.

"I wouldn't advise that," Jim said. "The whole advantage is to have these guys working at the same time while everything is opened up. The plumber may be drilling hole for pipes, and the electrician can come in right behind him and do his job. It makes a lot more sense to have it all done together."

I told Jim I agreed with that, but I still wanted a little time to think it over. He gave up the hard sell. "Take your time," he said. "I'll tell you what. I'm going to make this job a priority. I'll tell them not to take any other work until I hear from you. How 'bout that?"

"I appreciate it, Jim. I'll be sure to get back to you this afternoon."

As I was about to get into my truck, the third man who had sat with Austin and Ted walked up to me. "Mr. Head," he said. "I'm Austin's son. I work with him. I just want you to know that if you give us this work we'll do a really good job for you. And if you don't give us something this time, we do all kinds of work on houses other than plumbing. Here's a card so you don't have to go through Jim Gann to find us."

The business card read "Austin and Son," and listed their telephone number. I shook his hand and thanked him for the card.

I wouldn't be surprised if Jim saw through my "Let me think about it" line. I'm sure he's had lots of customers who play hard to get, or, at least, not easy to get. My call that evening to tell him he had the work couldn't have been unexpected. But he was as effusive as someone who had just gotten a job offer from out of the blue. "You won't regret it, John. We'll get this work knocked right out and I promise you'll be pleased with the result. When can we meet to sign the papers?"

"I'll be going down to the farm again first thing Saturday," I said. "Can we do it down there?"

"I'll be working somewhere else on Saturday," Jim said. "But tell you what. I'll send the papers down there with Austin on Saturday. You can go over it and sign it and give him the check for half."

"Sounds good to me."

"You won't regret it, John."

———

I felt my first hint of regret Saturday afternoon. No one had shown up by then. By the evening it was clear no one would.

I wasn't that upset about it, but this certainly wasn't the way I wanted things to start with them. When I called Jim Gann that night, he began the apologies as soon as he recognized my voice. "They were on their way down there first thing in the morning and that truck of theirs broke down and left 'em stranded on the expressway. I sent somebody over to try to get 'em goin' and they just couldn't. They expect they'll get down there and work all day Sunday."

But Sunday turned out to be another no-show day. The truck still refused to make the trip. I decided to try to be patient, like . . . well, like Job.

By Tuesday, when I drove down to the farm again, I had stopped worrying. I wasn't even concerned when I found no sign that they had been there Monday. I hadn't expected them to make their first trip down until I would be there to sign the contract and hand over the up-front money. In fact, I had reason to be glad they weren't there when I arrived. That meant I could finish my first attempt at committing carpentry without being under the watchful eyes of experts.

I was just about done tearing out the inside of the house, so I decided to get started putting things in. My first project was to put up studs for the interior walls of the downstairs bathroom and the laundry room, which would share a wall with the bathroom. I had begun the week before, thinking I would knock it out in a day or so. Here I was starting my fourth day of work on it, with no certainty it would be done when I left to go back to Atlanta.

But I enjoyed the work, as usual. There's something therapeutic about working with your hands. There's a kind of satisfaction and sense of accomplishment you rarely, if ever, get in an office. As a journalist, I can spend hours working on a story and at the end of the day know that what I've written hasn't finished the job. My work may just get it started, or it may just continue what someone else has started. And is my contribution good or bad? It depends on who you ask. And in the end, whose work is it, really? Mine alone? The editors along the way who are responsible for getting it into the paper? Or is it creation by committee?

There are no such questions when working with hammer and nails and wood. Your work is tangible and measurable. At the end of the day, you know if you've finished the job, and you know if you've done it right. It's your work, alone, and if you haven't done it well, you do it again until you've got it right. In the end, you feel you've accomplished something.

I feel those things in my soul when I'm working on the farm. For a brief time, I change my life, because I change my way of living. And it's not just a change of pace, either. Someone at the office said to me, "It must be great to just do things that don't require any thinking." That's wrong. Every job I do on the farm requires some thought, and most of them involve a mental challenge, figuring out the right procedure, as well as how to overcome obstacles and my own mistakes.

Take framing the bathroom walls, for example.

The floor still has a slight tilt to it, so the studs along one wall had to get longer as they approached the exterior wall. Getting it right was mostly a matter of measuring the space for each stud and then cutting it to fit. But the last one was more complicated. The

stud for the rough opening of the bathroom doorway had to rest
on the footing on the floor and fit snugly against the bottom of the
header that would rest on it. And when all the pieces were in place
they had to be squared so the door would fit and swing freely.

I carefully calculated the length of the stud I needed, taking the
footing and the header into consideration. As I measured and
marked the stud for cutting, I told myself that the worst thing I
could do was cut it too short. If it's too long, I told myself, you
have another chance to get it right. If it's too short, you're out of
luck. Three times I calculated, measured, and cut. Three times
the stud came out short.

What was I doing? I certainly wasn't thinking. I wasn't focusing
on the problem enough to come up with a solution. I decided to sit
and think about it for a few minutes. Weren't my calculations and
measurements accurate enough to eliminate errors? Maybe they
were too complicated. The more steps involved, the more possibilities for mistakes. There ought to be a simpler way to measure the
stud and get it right. Then I realized there *was* a simple, foolproof
way. I took a stud into the bathroom and placed the edge of one
end on the footing. I leaned the top of the stud against the header,
which already was nailed in place. I put a pencil mark on the stud,
even with the bottom of the header. I went an eighth-inch beyond
the mark to provide a margin of error. I made the cut at the mark.
Then I took the stud in and put it in place. It fit perfectly.

As I sat on the front porch basking in the glory of my accomplishment, a beat-up old truck and a car turned into the driveway.
Austin got out of the truck, followed by his son, who I later learned
was called A. T. Ted Watkins unfolded himself from the car, and
Jim Gann slid out of his tight fit behind the steering wheel.

"Here they are, like I promised, ready to go to work," Jim
said. "I told 'em they was goin' to get down here today if I had
to bring 'em myself. Well, as you can see. I brung 'em."

Austin and A. T. began taking tools and plumbing fittings out
of the truck. Ted walked around the house, taking a close look at
everything. I could see he was visualizing problems he might face
and calculating how to solve then. When he walked past me, he

turned, smiled, and said, "It sure is a long-assed way to come down here." Those were the first informal, almost friendly words Ted said to me.

The three men went right to work. Austin and A. T. spent a lot of time drilling holes in the floor for the plumbing. One would work underneath the house with the drill. The other was inside, making sure the driller was right on the mark. I enjoyed hearing their back and forth shouted in their Caribbean accents.

Ted found a radio and turned it on. He sang along, even when the heavy-duty drill he used to clear paths for the wiring in the floors, walls, and ceiling drowned out the sound of music. He gave special gusto to Motown music, and to the soul sounds of Memphis, which, I was told later, was the town where he grew up.

The trio joked back and forth, of course, with most of the banter at Ted's expense. During a break in the work, A. T. winked at me and said, "I call that big old mon Teddy Bear 'cause that's what his wife calls him." Ted laughed. "Aw, man," he said. "Shut up with that stuff." He took most of it in that good-natured way, but sometimes a barb struck something inside him. Then he turned silent and solemn.

There's something very pleasant about working with men. I enjoy the company of women. I like talking to anyone whose experiences are different from my own. But sharing physical work with other men can be special. Perhaps it would be the same if I spent time doing that kind of work with women. I'm not one to turn up my nose at "women's work." What we call women's work can be as hard and draining as any of the jobs men labor at. My mother raised and provided for five children on her own by doing "women's work." The strength it took for her to do that amazes me still. But men who work together with their hands and share the exertion that brings out sweat create a bond.

I felt that way with the men who joined me in working on the house, even though I didn't really work with them. In fact, I worked around them, making sure my projects didn't put me in their way.

That unspoken comradeship existed among us by the end of

that first day, when I said I had to head back to Atlanta and they said they would stay on and work into the night in order to get as much done as possible. I said I could make a run into town before I left and bring them something back if they wanted. The three men answered in unison. "Beer!"

So I drove to the nearby convenience store and bought a twelve-pack. They all seemed surprised when I brought back more than a six-pack, and when I refused to let them pay me. It was a ritual I repeated the next few times they were working while I was there. I came to enjoy it, and there was one evening I remember in particular.

It was the following weekend. Some minor setbacks had kept them from making the four-day deadline, but it was obvious they were making progress. They told me they'd be finished in just a couple of more days. I was in high spirits when I made the end-of-the-day beer run. I decided that before driving back to Atlanta, I would sit with them and have a soft drink while they had their beer. Everyone was in a good mood. Austin grew expansive while talking about the possibilities for the house.

"You can have a beautiful place out here, mon," he said. "You expand that bedroom to make it into a real big room. You put a deck out in the back with hot tub. And you build two apartments down there in the back. They pay for themselves in rent, pay for this house and give you a profit. And I do all the work. You don't have to worry 'bout no Jim Gann. We do every-ting."

A. T. nodded. "Every-ting, mon," he said.

"Let the man get finished with what he's doing before you start trying to talk him into doing something else," Ted said in a teasing voice that had an edge to it. He was being sensible, and that was what I planned to do in any case. But I didn't mind Austin's trying to talk me into giving him more work. His words seemed to float on ocean breezes. I was enthralled by the sound of his voice and the vision of the house he conjured.

I drove up the expressway that evening thinking a boundary had been crossed in that drinking session. I felt Austin and A.T., especially, didn't see me the way they saw me that first morning we met. I was no longer just the owner of a house they were working on under the auspices of Jim Gann. They knew I wasn't someone who would lord it over them and order them around. They saw that even while I was there with them, I didn't interfere with their work. I didn't constantly look over their shoulders to make sure they were doing it right. They knew I enjoyed having them around.

And that, I believe, was the problem.

+≻═ ═≺+

I lost patience with Jim Gann's crew after the "four-day job" stretched into four weeks and then continued inexorably toward four months. The contractors weren't just working slowly; they weren't working at all. Time and again I arrived at the farm and found no sign that they had been there. Even more infuriating, I sometimes found signs that they definitely had been there—fast food bags and wrappers, beer cans, cigarette butts—and no evidence that they had done any work. I thought they were mocking me.

Calls to Jim Gann did no good. "I'm sorry about this," he would say. "I saw 'em yesterday and they said they was almost done. I'll get on 'em. This shoudda been finished long ago. You been waiting long enough."

One call to Jim Gann was quickly followed by a call from A. T., Austin's son. "I apologize John," he said. "We planned to be done by now, but we got pulled off to some other jobs. We were down there today and just about got done. One more day of work and we should have everything ready for you to inspect."

I went down to do some work on the farm a couple of days later, a Friday. No more work had been done, and the job wasn't close to completion. This, I thought, is it. I had had enough. I would call Jim Gann and tell him to forget about trying to get Austin, A. T., and Ted to make an appearance. I didn't want them to do the work. Fed up, frustrated, and discouraged. That's how I felt. I walked around the house, trying to find some semblance of a home. I didn't see any. The walls weren't just bare, they were gutted. There was a rusted roof overhead, with no ceiling. It was only the middle of November, but the coldest night of the year was forecast. Even at midday, the chill wind whistled through the loose and missing wood siding. What I had known as a place of warmth and hospitality was as cold and inhospitable as Siberia.

The sun was almost down, the wind was up, and the temperature was dropping like a heavy stone crashing through the ice of a frozen pond. I was locking the front door, preparing to leave for Atlanta, when a car turned into the driveway. It was one of those big old cars left over from the days when gasoline cost less than fifty cents a gallon. Ted Watkins got out of the passenger side and called to me across the car's roof.

"Mr. Head!" he said. "I sure am glad I caught you. I been trying to find your phone number. I need to get in to finish the wiring and I ain't got a key."

We walked toward each other. Should I just tell him straight out that it was too late, that I had had enough and would hire someone else to do the rest of the work? I thought. "Where's Austin?" I asked. "Is he coming?"

"Naaw, I had to put them down," Ted said. "They didn't want to do right. They come to pick me up and tell me we're going down here to finish up. Then they say they got to stop some place to finish a little roofing job or put up some gutters or something like that. Sometimes they just stop by here on the way somewhere else just to pick up some tools or to have something to eat. I didn't have no other ride, so I had to go along with them. Then, the other day they come by and said, 'We're going down to Jackson to do that work. Come on.' And I said, 'You sure you're going this time? I'm almost through with the electrical.' They said, 'Yeah, we going. Come on.'

"So I went with 'em. First they want to stop for breakfast. They spent the whole morning sitting around the table bullshitting. That's all. I kept saying, 'Come on, we got to go and get this job finished.' Finally, we got in the truck and they start driving. I say, 'This ain't the way to go down to Jackson.' And A. T. said,

'We goin', but we got to stop and do a little job first.' And I said, 'Naaw, naaw, naaw. You'all don't need to do Mr. Head this way. Stop the car and let me out.' And A.T. says, 'What?' And I say, 'Stop this damned car and let me out.'

"So they let me out and drove off. I called my son and asked him if he could give me a ride down here and help me. He said he could come after he got off his job. So I came on down. We're planning to work all night and get done."

"I was going to tell Jim Gann I wanted to get someone else to finish the work," I said. "I think I've waited long enough. You can go ahead and do the wiring, but I'm going to find someone else to do the plumbing. If you see Austin, you can tell him that."

"I don't blame you one bit," Ted said. "I been trying to tell them they was going to lose this job. I said, 'The man ain't going to wait forever. He's trying to get this done.' But they wouldn't listen."

I gave Ted a key to the front door and a card with my telephone number on it. He had on a full-length down coat like the ones football players wear on the sidelines in freezing weather. I drove up the road wondering if Ted really would spend the rest of the evening working to finally finish the wiring. I couldn't help but think that he wouldn't. In dealing with contractors, I had learned, the only way to avoid disappointment was to hope for very little and expect nothing.

+━ ━+

The telephone rang the next morning. It was Ted. "Where are you?" I asked.

"I'm up the road from your house, using the neighbor's phone. I need you to stop by the store and get some switches and wiring I need to finish down here."

I said I would pick up the items on my way down.

"This old place sure got cold last night," he said. "I had to get up and put some plastic over places where the wind was coming in."

"You spent the night there?"

"Yeah, we didn't get finished last night and my son had to drive back up to Atlanta to go to work today. So I just stayed and worked as long as I could and then went to bed. I didn't know how cold it was until I stopped working. Man, I almost froze."

There was a mattress on the floor of the downstairs bedroom. It had only a couple of sheets and a blanket on it. I imagined Ted wearing his down coat, curled up in the covers and his teeth still chattering.

I could hear a rhythm-and-blues radio station when I arrived at the farm. It came from the old record player-radio console I had found in the house, the one that looked so decrepit I didn't even bother to plug it in. Desperate for company, Ted made it work and turned it up loud so he could hear it from anywhere in the house.

"I didn't know you were going to spend the night here with no heat and no water," I said.

"I just wanted to get everything done like I said I would," Ted said. "I got by last night. I must have put something over every hole in the walls, but it was still cold as a mother. But I did all right."

We worked at different jobs that day, mostly in different areas of the house, but, in a way, we were working closely together. I could always hear Ted's music, and sometimes Ted himself singing a sixties song. Once in a while Ted called me to help him with something. A couple of times I went to get food, which Ted ate with relish, since he had not eaten since the afternoon of the previous day.

Ted was still working when I left for Atlanta that evening. He said he expected to be done in a couple of hours and would call his son to come pick him up. "I appreciate you putting in the time to get this done," I said.

"I wouldda finished a long time ago if I could have," Ted said.

Jim Gann called the next day. "John," he said. "Ted just called me and said he's pretty much done with the electrical. He wants to know if you can come down there and do an inspection and if everything is satisfactory give him some money toward the amount due. We'll settle up on the whole thing later, but for some reason he really needs some money now. I know it's short notice, but could you take six hundred dollars cash down there to him?"

I told Jim I already had plans for the day, but could get the money and go down to the farm that evening. I asked if Ted mentioned that he spent two freezing nights in the house with no water and no heat so he could finish the work.

There was a pause on the other end of the line. "Well, bless his heart," Jim Gann said.

Well, bless his heart, indeed, I thought.

Ted had taught me a lesson. If you want to visualize a dream, if you want to conjure it up as easily as waving a magic wand, talk to someone like Austin, whose lilting voice and carefree ways allow you to see what might be. But if you actually want to get something done, seek out someone like serious, no-fun Ted Watkins. Find someone who's not afraid of work.

⊦⇒ ⇐⊣

I was in a foul mood while I waited for Jim Gann in the lobby of the *Atlanta Journal-Constitution* building downtown. It had nothing to do with the trials and tribulations of dealing with contractors. I was angry at Fate, which seemed to have turned against me big-time.

Jim had called the previous day and asked if we could meet at the Kentucky Fried Chicken in the morning and settle up for the electrical work. He also wanted to introduce me to the plumber who would finish what Austin started. I didn't put up a fight about paying for the rewiring despite our agreement that none of the balance would be paid until *all* the work was done. Ted Watkins earned his money. I wasn't going to hold it back from him because someone else let me down.

"And could you do me a big favor and bring the money in cash?" Jim asked. "I'd be happy to take your check, but for some reason Ted says he has to have his in cash."

I agreed to do it. I withdrew eighteen hundred dollars that afternoon, put it in an envelope, and put the envelope in my briefcase. After work that evening, I went to play tennis with a friend at courts in a toney part of town where we played almost every week. I parked my pickup, tossed my briefcase behind the seat, and went to the locker room to change into my tennis clothes. I brought my other clothes back to the truck, tossed them in, took out my tennis bag, and walked to the courts. I came back to the truck after the match, tossed the tennis bag in, and took my clothes and a towel to the locker room to shower and change again. It was dark as I walked toward the truck, but something on the ground beneath the passenger-side door glittered like diamonds in a street lamp's light. I felt the bottom drop out of my stomach and the top of my head float away at the same time.

Please don't let it be, I thought. Please don't let it be. Please, please, please. . . . It was.

The window had been broken. I looked inside. The tennis bag was gone. I said another little prayer before tilting the seat forward to look back there. My prayer wasn't answered. My briefcase was gone.

The police weren't sympathetic when I called. No officer would be sent to the scene. They took my telephone number and told me to go home and wait for someone to call to get information for a report. It wasn't until the call came and I was asked what had been stolen that I realized the extent of my loss. The money was bad enough ("How could you leave that much cash in your car?" the officer asked. "You probably made somebody's year."), but there also were notes on the work I had done on the house and what I had learned about its history. Worst of all, there was a manila envelope full of old photographs of my mother and her brothers and sisters on the farm and elsewhere. Those could not be replaced.

I called Jim Gann and told him what happened. He offered plenty of sympathy. He also wanted to know if I could get more money so he could at least make a partial payment to Ted.

"I can get the money," I said. "But I'll have to do it at my credit union at work. It opens at eight o'clock."

"Tell you what," Jim said. "We'll all come down there to meet you."

And so I fumed and waited until Jim Gann walked in with Ted Watkins and another man. "John, I'm sorry about what happened," Jim said. "That was terrible."

Jim waited until business had been taken care of before introducing the other man. "John, this is your new plumber, Bobby." he said. "Bobby, this is John Head."

Bobby the Plumber, I thought as we shook hands. He was perhaps in his late twenties, dressed in a work jacket, sweatpants, and high-top basketball shoes—the kind with stripes and colors and a steep price tag.

"You may have to drop some bread crumbs so I can find my way down there," he said. "I'm not too familiar with these places outside Atlanta and its environs."

"I'm going down there first thing Saturday morning," I said. "Why don't we meet and you can follow me down there?"

"OK. We can rendezvous at the KFC cattycornered from the stadium. I live in the vicinity."

Bobby the Plumber didn't show up Saturday morning. I went down to the farm alone. When I returned to Atlanta, I got his number from Jim Gann and gave him a call.

"What happened this morning?" I asked.

"A party that owes me compensation has reneged on his obligation. So I had to stay close by to monitor the situation and to ensure that he doesn't abscond."

This guy either went to Yale or served a long stretch in jail, I thought. If he went to Yale, he was trying to get his money's worth out of the vocabulary he picked up there. If he had been behind bars, he had followed the example of Malcolm X, who said he spent part of his time in prison learning every word in a dictionary.

I finally got Bobby the Plumber and a helper to come to the farm the following Saturday. They went to work in the front yard digging a trench for the new pipe from the meter to the house. I went around back to remove more vinyl siding from the house.

About ten minutes later, the helper jogged around the corner. I guess Bobby the Plumber wanted someone who could say things simply and in few words to give me the news. "He thinks he hit the main," the helper said.

When I went around front I saw a geyser rising up near the water meter. "They fooled me," Bobby the Plumber said. "The line wasn't supposed to come into the meter the way it did."

I called the water department to report the damage. The woman said she would send a crew out right away. I imagined an hour of waiting while water gushed into the air. And I was sure that when the crew finally arrived they would order the plumbing work stopped until I hired someone who knew what they were doing. But the county fooled me again. The crew showed up in about five minutes, fixed the pipe in ten, and then they were gone.

That episode didn't exactly inspire confidence in Bobby the Plumber. But I just wanted to get it over and done. He and his helper were still working when I left. The work would be done by the middle of the next week, he said. He would call me to let me know when he was ready for me to inspect the work.

He called Monday night. The work was done, he said. The pipes had been pressure-tested, and he found no leaks. So I went down the following day and looked at what he had done. But what was I looking for? I knew nothing about plumbing. All the pipes led somewhere. It looked OK to me. I just wanted an end to the plumbing work. So I met Bobby the Plumber at the KFC the next day to pay him. He had very little to say, except "Pleasure doing business with you."

When I went back down to the farm that weekend, I did what I should have done before. I turned on valves on all the lines. The pipes had more leaks than Ken Starr's office. Some of the connectors on the plastic pipe hadn't even been glued.

This was too much. Remember Job? He found himself covered head to toe with boils and sores sitting naked on an ash pile. I felt the way Job must have felt, only more depressed.

I walked around bearing that burden for a while. The weight must have been obvious when Chet Fuller, a friend and colleague, stopped me as I walked out of the office on a dark December day. "What's the matter, John?" he said. "You look like somebody died."

I told Chet my long and woeful tale—the contractors, the break-in, the money, the pictures, the notes, Bobby the Plumber. I told it all.

He listened. Then Chet said, "Cheer up. It's almost the end of the year. A new year is coming. Everything changes. Maybe something good is going to happen soon."

I didn't believe it for a minute. But Chet was right. Something good did happen. His name was Ben Hamilton.

CHAPTER 6

Ben Hamilton appeared on a bleak December day. A steady drizzle was falling, heavy rain was forecast, and the roof at the front of the house was open. I had peeled back the tin at the front edge of the roof ridge. For some reason, the house had been built with virtually no roof overhang at the front or back. This was why the wood siding and the studs in the exterior walls were in such terrible condition. Any hard rain not only sent water down the roof and over the side, it also splashed over the front and back edges. That rain ran straight down the siding, which made water damage inevitable. The problem was compounded when the vinyl siding was put on. After that, the water didn't just drip down the wood. It was trapped behind the vinyl, where it pooled. And the vinyl siding kept out the sun's drying rays. It was a formula for wood rot.

The roof needed overhang. I came up with a way to create it. I nailed two-by-fours along the edges of the roof in the front and back. Then I nailed one-by-six boards to the two-by-fours so the board extended out from the roof. The six-inch overhang would prevent water from running straight down the front and back of the house. Ted Watkins came down one weekend to help me put up the overhang in the back. We worked for two full days to do it, but we finally got it done. I was proud of it when we finally finished.

On that December day when the air was heavy with rain, I tried alone to duplicate what Ted and I did in the back. The struggle to get a twelve-foot-long two-by-four nailed along the roof line had taken all morning. It was clear I would never get the job done and the roof closed before the rain came. And the window installer was antsy to get his work done. After putting him off several times because I hadn't finished rebuilding the frames for the windows, I agreed to let him come down from Atlanta to measure the rough openings over the weekend. To top it all off, I found more problems when I made further checks of Bobby the Plumber's work. I decided not to call him back for fixes, figuring I had paid him for about as much damage as I could afford. Christmas was a week away, but I was in no mood to celebrate.

The first words Ben spoke to me didn't make me feel any better. "You think you got enough planks up there to keep from falling?" he asked.

It was gentle, good-natured teasing, but I couldn't take it that way. I had constructed an elaborate stacking of wood blocks and scaffolding until it was level with the porch roof's ridge. Then I used ten-foot-long two-by-twelves to bridge the gap between roof ridge and scaffolding, creating a catwalk from which work on the main roof could be done. My walkway consisted of four of the thick, wide planks—two stacks of two. I looked down on Ben. I was perhaps twelve feet above where he stood at the bottom of the porch steps. I could see he had spoken with a smile on his lips and in his eyes. "I had to figure out a way to bring it up here even with the top of the porch roof," I said in undue seriousness.

"I know," Ben said, still smiling. "But you could have done just fine with one plank up there. It wouldn't go anywhere."

"Well, better safe than sorry," I said defensively. Ben's jibe had hit a tender spot. I was nervous about working on the scaffolding, even at that modest height. It already had collapsed under me once, when I was working on the back of the house about twenty-five feet up. The network of steel pipes tilted away from the house and seemed to slowly dismantle itself in mid-air. The only reason I didn't fall into the middle of the crashing metal was that I managed to jump halfway through an upstairs bedroom window, like the reverse of a lover escaping an enraged husband.

So every possible precaution was built into my perches from then on—extra blocks underneath, two-by-fours to prop it up, ropes tied to scaffolding and snaked through windows. They looked like Rube Goldberg machines, but the purpose was to prevent them from falling down, not to make their collapse an entertaining spectacle. The one I was working on when Ben showed up used just one plank for a walkway at first. But it felt a little springy as I stepped across. I was frightened I might fall from the narrow path or that the plank's movement might cause the scaffolding to tumble. I was ashamed of my fear. Ben's comments struck into the heart of my embarrassment. That put me on guard against him.

"Come on in," I said. "I'll come downstairs." I crawled through the opening that had been one of the upstairs bedroom windows at the front of the house. Ben was standing inside the front door studying the gutted walls of the living room when I got there. He looked to be in his early fifties, maybe, and my height—about six feet tall. His face was dark and unlined, his hair neatly trimmed and black. I extended my hand. "Hi, I'm John Head," I said.

"I know," he said. "I'm Ben Hamilton. I talked to Myrtle a few days ago. She told me about what you're doing and said you needed some help. I told her I'd come out and take a look and see what I could do."

Weeks before, Mom had mentioned a friend who "worked on houses" and might be able to help me. Now he had deigned to show up and see if I was worthy. I was liking this man less and less by the minute. But I loved my mother too much to show disrespect or animosity toward one of her friends. And I was too desperate to let a bad first impression make me rebuff an offer of help. "I can use any and all the help I can get," I said.

Ben looked around the room again. "You done all this by yourself?" he asked.

"I opened up the walls and the ceilings myself. I had a contractor do some repair work on the foundation and the rewiring and replumbing."

"You get somebody from around here to do the work?"

"No, I talked to some local folks but couldn't find anybody willing to do the work. I wound up getting a contractor from Atlanta to come down and handle it."

"I wish you had come to me first," Ben said. "Probably could have saved you some money."

I wanted to tell him I didn't know who he was, much less that I could go to him about advice about anything. Instead I held my tongue.

"Do you mind if I look around to see what's you've done so far?" Ben said.

"Sure."

A mostly silent tour of the house followed. Ben simply looked closely at everything. "Hmmmm," was about as talkative as he got while he studied the wiring, plumbing, and my carpentry. But I could almost hear his critical thoughts. I made a comment now and then to show that I hadn't been fooled by the plumber and knew he'd made a mess of things. Or I might say something in defense of the framing I had done if Ben lingered a little too long looking it over.

We ended the tour in the front bedroom upstairs. Ben stood with one foot on the bottom rung of a stepladder, his hands resting on his bent knee. He had a way of tilting his head sideways to let you know he was about to ask a question. "Do you mind if I tell you what I think?" he said. "Some people just want to do everything the way they want to do it. They don't want to hear what anybody else has to say. If you feel like that, I won't waste your time."

"No, no. I want to hear anything you've got to say. I never mind listening to what somebody else has to say."

"That's good," Ben said. He was quiet for a moment. "I really like what're you're doing. I think it's a good thing that you're fixing up your granddaddy's house. It's good that you have so much respect for what he did. A lot of people don't care about stuff like this. And the wiring and plumbing work look OK. There's one or two things I might have done different, but that's no biggie. But it looks like to me that you're getting ahead of yourself."

"What do you mean?"

"All this wiring and plumbing work could have waited. You needed to get this roof taken care of first thing. You did the right thing by taking down the walls and the ceiling, but you ought to do everything you want to do while the ceiling and everything are open. Once you got everything closed up, it's too late. You are planning on a new roof, aren't you?"

"I'm trying to decide what to do about the roof. I'd like to keep it if I can. I've checked on some coatings that could be used to preserve it."

"Why do you want to keep this rusty old roof?"

"I just like the idea of having the tin roof on the house." There was more to it than that, of course. The sound of rain on a tin roof was a favorite part of the soundtrack for my childhood memories. I wanted to hear that cacophonous drumbeat during a downpour and to fall asleep to the lullaby played by a gentle night rain. I wanted to hear those sounds again; I wanted my sons to experience it the way I did. That was left unsaid, though. It was too sentimental to share.

Ben smiled. "You know what it would look like to me if you do all this work and spend all this money to fix up the house and then leave the tin roof on it?" he asked. "It would look like a man who bought himself a brand-new suit of clothes and then puts on a raggedy old hat. Do you see what I mean? The way I see it, it wouldn't look too good."

"Well, I'm not wedded to the idea of keeping the roof," I said, feeling on the defensive again. "I'm still trying to decide."

"I'm just telling you what I think. It's your decision. What you do is up to you. Like I said, some people don't like to hear it."

"I'm always willing to listen to advice. I may not take it. If I disagree with it I'll tell you why."

"That's the way I like it," Ben said. "If that's the way you feel, we can work together. I'll help you as much as I can because Myrtle asked me and because I believe in what you're doing. I'll give you as much time as I can when I can, and I'll stick with you until I've done as much as I can do."

"I'd appreciate any help you can give," I said. "And I'll pay you for your time."

"Don't worry about money. That's not what this is about. Let's get the work done first. We can sort out anything about money after that."

"That's fine," I said.

"I'm leaving town for the holidays tomorrow," he said. "I'm going to South Carolina to see my daughter. I'll be back after New Year's. We can get started then."

Ben stopped as we walked down the stairs. "When was this house built?" he asked.

"It was finished in 1940."

"That means it was brand new the first time I was inside here. That's been fifty-seven years ago?"

"You were in this house in 1940?"

"Yeah. I must have been—what?—six or seven years old when I first came inside this house. We lived in a house right up the road there. I used to come over here to play with Doris and Marvin. We were all just little kids, but I called myself being Doris's boyfriend."

I felt myself softening toward Ben. There were connections between us now. He had known the house in its infancy. He knew my mother and my aunts and uncle when they were children. There were questions I wanted to ask him. He might know other things I wanted to know. I had reasons to look forward to working with Ben Hamilton.

I walked with Ben to the gray van he had parked in the driveway behind my pickup truck. A plate on the front bumper had the word "RETIRED" in the center. Surrounding that, in the four corners of the plate, were the phrases "No Mortgage," "No Paycheck," "No Boss," and "No Worries." I had a moment's worry about what I was doing by bringing Ben Hamilton into my dream. Maybe he was one of those retired folks with time on his hands and nobody to boss around. He struck me as somebody who was used to being in charge. Perhaps he planned to take charge of the house renovation. "We'll see," I told myself after Ben left. "We'll see."

+≽— —≼+

New Year's Eve was going to be the coldest night of the winter so far, but I wanted to greet the New Year inside the farm house anyway. I was told growing up that the first day of the year set the tone for the year to come. The person you were with on New Year's Day would be the person you'd be with for the rest of the year. The things that occupied you on New Year's Day would occupy you throughout the year. I would wake up alone in a drafty, unheated house with exposed plumbing that probably wouldn't work because of frozen and burst pipes. But there was something symbolically important in spending that night on the farm. It was worth the risk of preordaining myself to an unpleasant 1998.

Mom thought my determination to spend the night in the farmhouse wasn't very smart. She feared she would find her eldest son on New Year's Day frozen solid, just like the plumbing. Despite my assurances that I would be fine, that I had space heaters and a sleeping bag guaranteed to keep me toasty and comfy in temperatures down to thirty below zero, she insisted on bringing an extra quilt for the bed. Even when their children move into middle age, mothers continue to believe they don't know how to keep warm.

Darkness had fallen and the temperature had dropped below freezing by the time I arrived at the farm early in the evening. I'm not much of a New Year's Eve person. I don't spend the day looking back or the night partying at fast-forward speed until midnight. So I didn't want to listen to the radio to hear people reflecting on the events of 1997 or playing the hits of the last twelve months as a musical countdown to 1998. I simply spent a couple of hours rearranging the chaos inside the house.

While working in the downstairs bedroom, I saw the night sky through a window. It was crammed full of stars. Each had a brightness as sharp as a laser. It reminded me again of how different—how much more beautiful—a clear night sky is out in the country away from the city and the ubiquitous man-made lights that dim the heavens.

I had wriggled into my sleeping bag in the back bedroom upstairs by 9:00 P.M. The house was quiet. The only noise was the infrequent passing of cars on the road out front. Stray light from the automobiles' headlights made patterns that moved across the bedroom ceiling, just as it had during the many nights I spent in that bedroom as a child. I could see the sky through a window from my bed. Again, I was mildly amazed by its beauty. Feeling at peace, I soon was asleep.

Something woke me up. I didn't know what time it was, but I sensed the New Year had arrived. It wasn't because I heard any midnight revelry. Down in Butts County, out in the country, the sophisticated, citified idea of making as much racket as possible to scare away the evil spirits of the old year had not yet taken hold. Many people there own guns, of course. Some fire them every day, shooting at game or at targets. But they don't waste bullets once a year by shooting into the air at midnight. My awakening had not come with a sudden jolt of noise. Rather, I was drawn to a slow, gentle emergence from sleep by sounds I wanted to hear.

I heard cows lowing in the pasture across the road. There also was the rumble and horn-blowing of a train on the tracks less than a half-mile away. These were two more reminders of my childhood on the farm. The sound of the train had a particular resonance. It made me think of the child I had been, the child who heard the trains and wondered where they had been and where they were going, and then wondered if he would ever go to such places.

My aunts and uncles must have had the same thoughts when they were children sleeping within earshot of passing trains. They must have envisioned the big cities the trains traveled to. They must have thought about seeing places far away from the farm.

In a cache of old pictures my mother pulled out of photo albums for me was a picture of my Uncle Chester during World War II. On the back, someone had written in a neat hand, "Chester in Europe." He sits in a smoky café with two other black soldiers. There is a bottle of wine and glasses on the table. Uncle Chester is at the center of the picture. He's in uniform, with his hair slicked back. He rakishly holds a cigarette in one hand. He looks like a sophisticate, not like the Georgia boy he was, the refugee from the farm fields who no doubt still had red clay clinging to his shoes. I'm sure the war took him and his brothers to places they never imagined they would see.

If I traveled farther and reached higher than my aunts and uncles, it was because I stood on their shoulders. That's how one generation rises above the one before. My paths were paved by the work and sacrifice of people like Uncle Chester on behalf of their country and their people—and when I say "their people" I mean both those they were bound with by race and those they were connected to by blood. What they gave allowed me to go to places they never dared dream of, even when they fell asleep to the sound of trains.

I awoke early in the morning. It was still freezing cold, but it felt good to be in the house on the first day of the year. Water had frozen in the toilet bowl. I tried the faucets in the sink. Nothing came out. Leaving the water dripping had not prevented the pipes from freezing. I would have to wait for the thaw to see if any had burst.

There was work I wanted to get started on before going to my mother's house. I began sorting through the wood I piled up outside while gutting the house. Lumber that might be reusable had to be separated from the rotted, insect-damaged wood that would be thrown away. Then the prized tongue-and-groove—destined for use as flooring and on cabinets—had to be set aside. As I picked through and lifted the wood, I was again struck by how much more heft the "old" wood from the house had compared to the "new" wood I was using for repairs. It made me wonder for a moment if I was somehow weakening the house instead of repairing it. But I knew that wasn't so. The repairs had to be made. The wood being taken out, even the wood that was still in good shape, was part of something that had served its purpose for as long as it could.

When Mom opened her door, she said, "I guess it's going to be a good year. They say if a good man comes to your house on New Year's Day it brings good luck."

"Does that mean you're expecting a good man to come by later?" I said.

"Ahhh, don't say that," she laughed. "You're the best man I expect to see today and for the rest of the year."

I got that kind of pampering most of the day, including being treated to a traditional Southern New Year's Day dinner: black-eyed peas and rice so the year would be filled with coins, and collard greens to add folding money. Thank goodness Mom left out the chitlins, which are supposed to bring silver.

After dinner I went back to the farm for more wood sorting. It was almost nightfall when I decided to head back up to Atlanta. For the first time that day, I allowed myself to reflect on the past year, focusing on the farm. Almost a year had passed since the bank approved our mortgage application and James and I knew we would soon own the property. Six months had passed since I began work on the renovation. As I walked around the house in the failing light, it was difficult to see that very much had been done toward saving the house. Sure, the foundation was sound now, but that soundness was as hidden from view as the rot had been. Gutting the interior and removing the siding from the outside revealed more damage and flaws. The debris piled everywhere, both inside and outside the house, made the place look like a junkyard, not like a home where someone would want to live. All in all, it was a discouraging sight. It was enough to make me doubt that I had accomplished very much in a year's time.

Yet I did have a very real sense of accomplishment. Yes, there was so much more to be done. But in every corner there was something that had been done, something I did myself to make the house better—a new wall in the bathroom, new framing for windows, rotted studs pulled out and replaced. And everywhere there were reminders of the things I had learned about the house and the people who lived in it. There were books and bottles and pages and coins and other items of everyday life that turned up inside walls, under floorboards, and in closets. There were the names of the carpenters who signed their work before the walls were sealed. The house was telling me its stories, and I was listening.

I took one more look at the house as I got into my truck. The time spent here during the year has been worthwhile, I thought. I got things done. I enjoyed it. All I could ask for was for the coming year to be as good.

⊱ ⊰

Ben was back by the first weekend of the New Year. He was already at work upstairs when I arrived that Saturday morning. Studs for the wall and the doorway of the front bedroom were nailed in place.

"Happy New Year, young fella!" Ben wielded a hammer with his left hand, pounding in another nail.

"Happy New Year to you," I said. I studied the work he had done. "Looks like you've been busy."

"I like to get started early," Ben said. "I'm following the floor plan you left for me, but I've got some questions to ask you."

We went from room to room, with Ben pointing out discrepancies between actual measurements and the dimensions on my floor plan. A window might be six inches off one way or another in the drawing. Ben said he would have to make adjustments as he went along. He just wanted to make sure that was OK with me.

And then Ben led me outside and around to the back of the

house. "What's this?" he asked, putting his hand on the new floor I had built over what had been the back porch.

"That's going to be a breakfast room," I said. "I'm going to glass it in."

"Have you already ordered the windows?"

"No. I'm just planning to have plate glass."

"What about a door?"

"It'll be over there on the back side."

"How big is this room going to be?"

I didn't like the way this grilling was going. "It's ten feet by nine feet."

"You think that's going to be big enough to put a table with some chairs around it, and have room for a door where you can come in?"

"I think so."

"You'd be surprised how much space a table and some chairs can take up," Ben said. The skepticism was evident in his voice. "And what's this supposed to be?" he asked, pointing to the ledge I had created with two-by-twelves that extended the floor on three sides.

"I added that to give it a little more space," I said.

"What's holding it up?"

"These," I said, pointing to the four-by-fours that had been bolted to the sill and to which the floor extensions had been bolted.

"I don't think that's going to be enough," Ben said. "You're going to have a wall sitting on top of that, and a roof resting on the wall. With all that pressure you know what's going to happen, don't you? Over time, that wood is going to curl down. A building inspector is going to take a look at that and say it won't work. I don't think he'll pass it."

My grand design for a room that looked as if it floated on air and defied gravity was being shot down. Ben knew rooms don't float on air and that gravity is not defied. Building inspectors know it too, which is why they don't let amateur architects create rooms that might fall down on people. But I was stubborn. I

wanted to make this wonder work. "I'm going to add more support," I said. "I'm going to cut more two-by-twelves and nail
them at an angle underneath here. That should hold it up."

"I'm not sure I'm getting what you're planning," Ben said.
"Have you got drawing of it."

"No," I said. "I'll do some sketches for you."

"OK," Ben said. "I just need to see what you're trying to do."

We were inside the house again, upstairs, discussing Ben's
other ideas about work that should be done. But I was distracted
by an uneasy feeling. I was beginning to wonder if I was letting
Ben take over the restoration that was supposed to be *my* mission.
Was I too deferential toward him and his ideas? Should I be more
assertive in maintaining my vision of what the house should be?
Perhaps when he was shooting down my architectural innovation, I should have said, "By God, Ben. If I want a levitating
breakfast room, then I'll build a levitating breakfast room."

Just as I was thinking those thoughts, Ben cocked his head to
the side and got that inquisitive look in his eyes. "I bet you're
wondering why I'm doing this, aren't you?" he said.

"No," I said. "I understand that. . . ."

"No. You don't understand. You probably think I'm after
some money—going to do the work and then ask you for a lot
of cash in the end. But that's not it. It's got nothing to do with
money. Maybe you think I call myself being your mamma's
boyfriend. That's not it either. Myrtle just been a friend to me
and my family for a long time. Or you might think I just want to
come out here and take over, do everything the way I want."

Bingo, I thought.

"That's not it either. You want to know why I'm doing this?"

"Sure."

"'Cause I feel like I owe it to your granddaddy for what he did
for us. We were literally starving when we got here. I mean *starving to death*. I remember days when I went to school and the only
lunch I had was a pocket full of dry oatmeal. That's the truth.

"Buddy Fitch gave my daddy some work and he let him grow
food on a little piece of land. That saved our lives. I always said

I would pay him back if I ever got the chance. I figure helping
you with what you're doing here gives me a chance to repay
some of it."

I was amazed on two counts. First, I didn't know Grandpa was
capable of such generosity. But then I thought Grandpa must
have believed he was getting the best of the bargain based on the
work he would get out of Ben's father. But this happened during
the Depression, and any kind of work was a blessing. So, whatever his reasons, my grandfather had given something very pre-
cious to Ben and his family.

The second source of my amazement was Ben's insistence on
repaying a debt that was more than half a century old. He was
treating it the way debts were treated at the time this good deed
was done. There was no statute of limitations. Payment was eternally due, until the debt had been repaid in full.

Once again, Ben had told me something that softened my
heart toward him. We were bound together more closely than I
could have guessed. I was the beneficiary of a good deed done by
my grandfather almost sixty years ago. A circle has been closed, I
thought. I wondered how many more such circles I eventually
might find.

CHAPTER 7

I believe Ted Watkins fell in love with the house. It wasn't just a one-night stand—or even the two-night stand he needed to finally finish the electrical work. His affection was evident when I offered to pay him by the hour if he came down to help me work on the house. He began to talk about what the house might be. Maybe he already had seen it, but felt uncomfortable talking about it. Perhaps he was afraid I wouldn't take to it kindly, like a man who sees another guy trying to put the moves on his girl.

He asked me several times if I planned to live on the farm once the renovation was complete. I told him the same thing each time—that the house probably would be a place for weekends and other short stays. Ted found it hard to believe that I wouldn't move in.

"This is going to be a nice house when you're done," he said. "It don't take that long to drive up to Atlanta to work. You get your boys down here, they can go fishing and hunt. Have some animals, plant a garden, get some fruit trees going. You could have it all. I'd move down here in a heartbeat if I had this land and this house. Man! I don't see how you could beat it."

Ted opened up when we began working together without Austin and A. T. around. They weren't there to tease him or force him into the background with their overpowering personalities and Caribbean charm. We talked. Ted carried his end of the conversations and then some. A favorite topic was the houses he had done the electrical work on. He spoke of them like a man remembering the women he had loved. He found something memorable in each of them. There was the huge and exotic castle-like stone house that had more floor space in the attic than my family's entire farmhouse had. There was the elegantly modern mansion in Dallas, Texas. There was the ranch-style house in a rough Atlanta neighborhood that had been abused by renters. That was the house Ted pitied. He could see it had beauty once, but it had reached the point at which no amount of cosmetic work could make it attractive again. When I mentioned Ben's insistence that the tin roof should go, Ted was just as adamant in arguing that I keep it. Obviously, somewhere in Ted's past was an old house whose tin roof he slept under while rain fell.

The descriptive Ted used most often for the farm house was "old," and he always said it in a complimentary way. "This is a good old house," he would say. Or, "This old house is just fine." Or, "They built this old house to last."

Ted's feelings about the house had to do in part, I think, with his deep respect for wood. Sometimes he rubbed his hand gently along a stud or a rafter, as if stroking a prized pet. He treated as a worthy adversary the dense, dark rafters and sill timbers that had grown stronger with age. He avoided confrontation with them whenever possible. The easiest route between two electrical outlets wasn't always a straight line. "This old wood is hard as hell," he said. "Wore out two drills making holes for the wiring."

He admired wood's flexibility, and I use the word "flexibility" literally. Ted believed it would bend to his will. We were making a header for a door one day by putting two two-by-eights together. When the boards were nailed one on top of the other, we saw that one board was slightly warped. There were two spots—one at the top, one at the bottom—where the edges weren't even. Ted studied the boards. "This ain't going to fit right the way it is," he said. "Bring me some of those big nails. I'll straighten it out."

He held a nail tilted at an angle on the surface of the top board. He began hammering. The nail made its way through the top board and into the one on the bottom. When the head of the nail was flush with the top board's surface, Ted kept hammering. With each blow, part of the top board moved a fraction. The bow in the board disappeared. All edges of the two boards were even, and the header was ready to be installed. "I can't believe that worked," I told Ted.

"That ain't nothing," he said. "I've seen some carpenters take wood that's crooked as can be and make it straight. You'd be amazed what wood can do."

But he also could treat wood rudely. If we cut a piece of wood and found we had left it just a hair long, Ted hammered it into place anyway. He pounded round pegs into square holes, winding up with pegs that were a little more square and holes that were a little more round.

+═══ ═══+

The first time Ted agreed to go down to the farm to help me with the work, he asked me to pick him up near the Capitol Homes public housing project, a downtown neighborhood that's one of the city's toughest. It was a frigid early morning. Temperatures in the teens the previous night had set a record low. I left the pickup truck engine running and the heater on while I sat parked near the street corner where Ted was supposed to meet me. After fifteen minutes, there was no sign of him.

I drove around the area, thinking I might have misunderstood where we were to meet. After circling the block and arriving back at my original lookout point, I saw Ted running toward me. He wore that long down jacket of his and a knit cap. He had a tool belt that looked like a gun holster slung over his shoulder. Steam poured out of his body in the cold air.

"Man!" he said. "Didn't you hear me hollering at you? You was pulling off just as I was walking up. I thought you was going to leave me out here in the cold. I wasn't up for that. Already spent the night outside."

"You slept outside last night? What happened?"

"I was staying at my wife's apartment, right? Man! We split up and got back together so many times I lost count. I want to be there because my youngest boy is with her and he needs me. She can't really take care of him, can't get him to school, can't help him with his homework. At least I can do that, so I try to do that. But it seem like every time we get together something happens. She starts drinking and we get into a fight and she tells me to leave the apartment or she's going to call the cops. They come and arrested me one time even though I told them I was her husband and I'm the boy's daddy. But my name ain't on the lease, right? So I got no right to be there. We started fighting last night, so I just up and left. Didn't have anywhere else to go, but I damn sure wasn't going to stay there."

"Man!" I said. "You must have froze out here."

"Just about," Ted said. "I woulda froze, if I hadn't had this coat." Then he laughed a short, sharp laugh. "Three dudes tried to take it from me last night. I was walking down the street and all of a sudden they was standing in front of me. They was young-bloods, but big ones. One of 'em said, 'You gon' have to give up the coat.' I said, 'Naw, I can't do that. I need this coat.' Then they spread out around me so one of 'em was on each side. Man! I knew they was getting ready to jack me up. Then it just so hap-pen that a friend of mine come by and helped me run 'em off. I don't know what I woulda done, but I know they wasn't going to get this coat as cold as it was."

That morning revealed what I came to see as a pattern in Ted's life. He was constantly looking for a place to stay, and improvis-ing whenever he had to. Among the places I picked him up or dropped him off after a day at the farm were his friend's huge stone house that he admired so much, the apartment of a woman he had met at a party only a few days before, and a rental house the landlord let him live in while he did electrical work for her.

Through his many moves, Ted always called to let me know

where he was and to ask if I needed him to go with me to do
some work down at the farm. And he always was there at the
appointed hours when I came to get him. There was only one
time he didn't make it. I went to pick him up on a bitterly cold
Saturday morning at a large apartment complex. He was supposed
to meet me in front of one of the buildings at seven o'clock. He
wasn't there when I arrived. At seven-thirty he still wasn't there.
I had no telephone number for Ted. I didn't know which apartment he was in. I gave up and left after almost an hour had passed.

I knew Ted was working the night shift at a truck stop on
Atlanta's perimeter expressway. He was there from 3:30 P.M. to
1:00 A.M. He also worked wiring jobs whenever he could get
them during the week. Yet he always insisted that getting an early
start to go to the farm with me was no problem. Maybe the long
hours finally caught up with him and he overslept, I thought.

But Ted didn't call that day to explain what had happened. He
didn't call the next day either. That wasn't like him. I began to
worry that something might have happened to him.

I finally heard from him in the middle of the week. "John
Head, this is Ted Watkins," he said when I answered the telephone. Before I could ask him what happened that Saturday
morning, Ted explained.

"Man, I'm sorry about the other day," he said. "I woulda been
there, but I was in jail."

"Jail?"

"Yeah. This friend of mine gave me a ride home from work,
right? So he asked me if I wanted a beer. I said yeah and started
drinking it on the way. We was just about to turn into the apartment parking lot when this cop pulled us over. He got me for
having a open beer in the car. When he checked on me he found
I had a warrant out on me for a traffic ticket. He took me down
to the jail and I didn't get out until today, man."

That story might sound suspect to some people. I wondered, for
instance, what the people out at the truck stop thought about when
Ted explained why he had missed two nights of work. But I had
no doubt it was true. Ted had been too reliable and too anxious for

the work to not show up for no good reason. He kept apologizing for standing me up. I told him not to worry about it. Then he asked if I needed him to help me again the next weekend.

Ted worked with me just about every weekend. Invariably, he slept for most of the ride down to the farm and for most of the ride back up to Atlanta. But we made a ritual of stopping at a Shoney's restaurant for breakfast on the way down, and that gave us lots of chances to talk. Ted enjoyed telling me stories about growing up in Memphis. He told me about the time when he and his brother were on a boat on a river when a swarm of angry bees descended on them. Ted made it into the boat's cabin and locked the door before his brother could get in. "He had to go into the water, but he still got stung so many times," Ted laughed. "His face swoll up so much you couldn't even know him." And he told me about the time his father told him to take the roof off their garage. When his father came out to check on how the job was going, he found Ted sawing through the rafters. "Boy, what in the hell are you doing?" his father asked. "What you told me to do," Ted said. "I'm taking the roof off." "Not the whole roof," his father said. "I meant the shingles!"

Ted's father, who still lived in Memphis, seemed to be a strong influence in his life. He taught him about carpentry and doing other work with his hands. He gave Ted an appreciation of the outdoors during hunting and fishing trips down into Mississippi. And Ted inherited a love of all kinds of music from his father.

One morning, out of the blue, Ted asked me if I had seen the animated movie *The Lion King*. I told him I hadn't.

"You oughtta go see it," Ted said. "That movie is what it's all about. The circle of life. Everything you do comes back on you. All this stuff people doing is going to come back around. This New World Order. It ain't going to work."

I always thought "new world order" was a banality George Bush blathered on about to make himself sound like an international leader. But Ted told me it was a plot to control African Americans by putting as many young black men as possible in prison.

I hoped my complete skepticism didn't show. I knew it was

one of those beliefs that was beyond debate. I gave a noncom-
mittal grunt.

"Just go see *The Lion King*," Ted said. "You'll understand."

Sometimes I picked Ted up at one house in the morning, only to
have him tell me to drop him at another house where he would
spend the night. I never saw any evidence of his "moving"—
packing up his possessions and taking them from one place to
another. In fact, I didn't see any evidence that Ted owned much
beyond the work clothes he wore. His prized possessions were a
case full of tools. Some of them were specialized for his electrical
work. Others were everyday tools—a hammer, wrenches, a saw,
screwdrivers. The only time I ever heard Ted complain about his
nomadic lifestyle was when it caused him to lose most of his tools.

"I was staying with these guys and I had to go up to Memphis
for a visit," Ted told me. "They said they would keep my tools for
me. When I got back, they said they had put the tools in their
truck and somebody broke in and stole 'em. You think I believe
that? They know where my tools are. Yeahhh, man. They know."

We were on our way to the house where those "guys" lived
to pick up Ted's tool belt and the few small tools in it. He had
been told that those were the only things that weren't taken in
the break-in. As we turned a corner to the street where their
house was, we saw three police cars in the middle of the street.
The officers were out of their cars talking to each other. One of
them was writing on a clipboard.

"Stop here," Ted said as soon as he saw the cars. "Don't drive
close to the cops. I'll get out here and walk down to the house."

Ted walked past the police officers obviously avoiding eye contact, like a man who was afraid. He did the same on the way back.
I didn't blame him, given his past experiences with the police.

Ted got back into the truck. "Turn around and let's go," he
said. "I don't want anybody to see me around the cops and think

I'm a snitch. These guys around here don't put up with no snitches."

So it wasn't the police Ted feared. It was the crooks. The police might lock him up, but the drug dealers, or whoever the police were after, might kill him.

Incidents like that made me realize how different Ted's world was from mine. I never drove more than fifteen minutes from my house to wherever Ted was staying, but I might just as well have traveled a million miles. I knew from the stories Ted told me about his childhood that he and I grew up in similar circumstances, with the major difference being that Ted's father was at the center of his family and my father was absent. But despite those analogous beginnings, our paths through life had moved in different directions. The farm house brought us together, and it kept us together longer than otherwise would have been possible. There were wide gaps between us by just about every measure. I could scoff at his fear of a conspiracy to lock up black men. I hadn't spent a moment behind bars in my life.

It reminded me of something that had been in the back of my mind ever since Ben Hamilton told me the story of how Grandpa saved his family from starvation. Generosity simply was not a concept I easily associated with my grandfather. I couldn't help but wonder if he might have taken advantage of the desperation of Ben's family; I wondered if he might have exploited them.

But could I talk, really? What about my relationship with Ted? Who was in a better position to exploit, my grandfather or I? In fact, the economic disparity between Ted and me probably was greater than that between Grandpa and Ben's father. Ben's family was dirt poor, but in the Depression era, the only thing that put my grandfather above them was his ownership of land. Even in these times of economic boom, however, the gap between Ted and me is wider—not just in terms of income, but also in terms of prospects. Ted has skills that always will allow him to earn money. But the time has come when wiring the house pays less than wiring the people—getting their PCs up and working and plugged into the Internet. The question is whether Ted and hard-working people like him will make the adjustment, or even be given a fighting chance to adjust.

The same information industry that is driving the economy to new heights is leaving a lot of people behind.

I remembered a couple of things that happened not long after I started working on the farmhouse. The first began when I was awakened from a nap between projects. I heard someone calling out, "Hello! Is anybody in there?" I looked out of the second floor window. There was a short, heavyset woman in blue jeans and a work shirt walking around the house. "Anybody here?" she called out again.

"I'm up here," I said. She looked up. "I'll come down."

When I walked out the front door the woman was standing in the yard with a young man who had the beginnings of a beard. "Sorry to bother you," the woman said. "We was driving by and saw all this wood you got piled up here. Decided to stop by and see if you was going to have it hauled away or what."

She was talking about the wood I had discarded while gutting the house. "I'm going to haul it to the dump eventually," I said.

"Well," the woman said, "we was wondering if you mind if we pick out some of the wood to use for a house we're building down the road there."

"Sure," I said. "Help yourself."

"We'll go get the van and come pick it up," the woman said. She took out a piece of paper. "Would you mind writing a note that says you give us permission to take some of the wood? And sign it and put your phone number down. If the sheriff comes by and sees us taking some wood, we want to show him we ain't stealing it."

The second episode happened when I took debris to the county dump. There were three large containers people could toss their trash into. As I drove up, I noticed a young man and woman standing on top of the heap in one of the containers. Their children—I think there were three—sat in what looked like a fairly new van, while the couple picked through the garbage, setting aside the few things they could use out of the thousands of things other people had cast away.

I wondered why the two couples were scavenging. Why, in a time of plenty, were there people getting by on leftovers that fall

from the higher layers of the economy? Conditions in America
were as far removed from the misery of the Depression as they
ever had been. Yet, there were people like Ted who were working two jobs and still barely getting by.

I know Ted was grateful for the money he made working with
me. He told me so more than once. But was I paying him what his
labor should be worth? I'm sure of one thing. In his day, my grandfather paid more to Ben's father than I could ever pay Ted. In
exchange for his labor, Grandpa helped a man get his dignity back.

⊹━ ━⊹

Ted met Ben Hamilton on the second Saturday in January. Ben's
van was already in the driveway by the time Ted and I arrived.
We found him working upstairs. He had a Skilsaw in his left hand
and held a two-by-four in his right. He quickly sawed through
the pencil mark he had made on the wood. Another stud was
ready for the wall he was framing. He had already framed the
doorway and put up studs for the front wall of the bathroom.

"Well, well. Look who's here," Ben said. "I've been working
for an hour already. I thought you said you got started working
early on Saturdays."

Ben was teasing me again. I looked at my watch. It was a little
after eight o'clock. I smiled at him. "Ben Hamilton," I said, "this
is Ted Watkins. He's the electrician who did the wiring for me."

The two men shook hands. "Did you take a look at the
wiring?" Ted asked. "Everything look all right to you?"

I held my breath. I knew Ben would be blunt. If there was
something about the wiring he didn't like, he would say so. I
didn't want him to start things off on an unpleasant note.

"Looks like to me you done all right," Ben said. "There was
one or two things that I might have done different, but that's no
biggie. Where did you learn electrical work?"

"In the army," Ted said.

"You were in the service?" Ben asked. "I was in the air force."

That gave them something to swap stories about for a while. They talked about postings around the world, about ranks, about making specialist and E-6. They compared the cultures of the two military branches. "I made master sergeant," Ben said. "A master sergeant in the army wasn't nobody. The air force treated master sergeants like kings." Ted nodded in agreement.

Ben looked to me when there was a lull. "Come on," he said. "I've got a few things to show you."

The three of us walked through the house. Ben pointed out things he thought weren't done correctly. Bobby the plumber had put up studs for the upstairs bathroom wall where the pipes for the bathtub and shower came up through the floor. He had spliced together some of the two-by-fours in a way that Ben said wouldn't do. Ben said he would replace those. The frame for the French doors to the kitchen wasn't plumb, he said. There were a few more minor things he noted.

Then Ben led me and Ted outside and around to the back of the house. He pointed to the roof. When I looked up I saw that the overhang Ted and I improvised and struggled for days to put up had been torn down. It had been replaced by what looked like new rafters that provided an overhang of about eighteen inches, instead of the six-inch overhang we had come up with. What Ben had done by himself was far superior to what Ted and I had done together.

"You got to have some overhang to keep the water off the siding," Ben said. "And it makes the roof line look better. I see a house that's just straight up and down like this one was, it looks like it's not finished yet."

"Looks good," I said.

Ted didn't say a word.

Ben left for dinner late in the afternoon. He said he would be back. Ted and I worked on for another hour, until it was time to take Ted back to Atlanta to go to work at the truck stop.

"So, what do you think of Ben?" I asked.

"He sure does know a lot," Ted said.

I think he meant it as a compliment.

+⇥= ⇥=+

It was soon clear that the help Ben was giving me made Ted's work unnecessary. After everything Ted had done for me, it was difficult to tell him that, basically, he was being replaced. So I fudged things a little.

"I'm going to be doing some things I can handle by myself with a little help from Ben," I told him. "I don't think I'll have enough for you to do to make it worth your time to come down for a while."

"That's cool," Ted said. "No problem."

It was a Saturday, and I was dropping Ted off at the house he was living in in exchange for doing electrical work for the owner. After he got out of the truck, Ted leaned back in through the passenger side window. "If you ever need me to give you some help, just let me know, even if you don't have any money to pay me," he said.

"Thanks Ted. I appreciate that."

"I'm serious as a heart attack," Ted said insistently. "I mean it, now."

"I believe you, Ted."

And I did.

Ted didn't come down to work on the house again. I spoke to him on the telephone a few times. The last time he called and asked to borrow some money. "This electrical job I had fell through. I just need a little something to keep me going. I'll pay you back as soon as I get some work."

I lent Ted the money. I wasn't worried about being paid back. I knew he would repay me as soon as he could.

Months went by without my hearing from him again. One day I decided to try the last phone number I had for him. The number had been changed. The new number was unlisted. That meant Ted wasn't there. The telephone had never been in his name in the first place. And Ted was too practical to pay extra for *not* being in the phone book.

I hope he found a good place to stay.

CHAPTER 8

"What holds a house together?" Ben Hamilton asked.

I knew it was a trick question, because the answer was so obvious and because Ben looked at me with that mischievous tilted head, arched eyebrows, and small smile he took on when asking a simple question that he fully expected would stump me.

"Nails?" I answered/asked, stepping timidly into Ben's trap.

"That's what people think," Ben said with satisfaction, his trap sprung. "They see something crooked, looking like it might fall off or fall down—bam, bam, bam, bam—they hammer in more nails and think they fixed it. But nails won't do it. Nails don't hold the house together. Pressure does—having one thing stacked on top of another, with gravity pulling down and pressing them together. That's why you want everything that carries a load to be plumb, straight up and down. You get gravity pulling everything the same way, they stay together. If it's out of line, gravity pulls one thing one way and the other thing another way. That happens, all the nails in the world won't hold them together. Eventually, those nails will be pulled out, and everything falls apart."

"I see what you mean," I said. "While I was gutting the house,

sometimes I found nails sticking out, like they had worked themselves out of the wood."

Ben smiled like a teacher satisfied that a slow student has
grasped a complicated concept. "Come over here," he said. "Let
me show you something."

We were in the front bedroom upstairs. Ben walked into a corner. I followed him. He pointed straight across the exterior wall
at the front of the house. "Sight along this wall and tell me what
you see," he said.

I looked along the wall whose tongue-and-groove planks had
been stripped away, laying bare the studs like the bones of a
butchered animal. Try as I might, I saw nothing to remark on,
even though I knew I surely should. "Looks OK to me," I said.

"Look again," Ben said. "Look at the studs below the top plate
and the ones above it. Are they straight up and down?"

The "top plate" consisted of two two-by-fours laid one on top
of the other. They rested on the studs that came up from the
floor. The top plate for this wall was only a little more than six
feet above the floor. Another set of studs rested on the top plate
and rose to rafters that rested on them. When I followed Ben's
hint and concentrated on the studs below and above the top plate,
the problem was as plain as could be. The studs were not straight
up and down. Both sets leaned out slightly. The walled looked
like a piece of paper that had been folded across the center and
then almost flattened again, but not quite.

"The wall's not straight," I said. "It's bulging out."

"That's right," Ben said. "Whoever built the wall tried to take a
shortcut. They didn't use studs long enough to have just one set that
went all the way up to the roof. They made two sets of short studs
and put one on top of the other. But they didn't get them straight.
It leaned out a little from the start, but it was too small to even see
back then. But over the years it moved out a little more at a time.
Now you can see how far it's gone. And if you don't do something
about it, it's going to keep going and you'll lose the wall."

Lose the wall? I imagined a literal house of cards. The front
wall would fold, and the rest of the house follow. This, I thought,

would not be good, unless I wanted to introduce a new architectural concept—the open-air bedroom.

"Are we going to have to replace the studs?" I asked. Ben probably knew some technique of putting a new stud right next to an old one. As soon as the new one is in place, the old one is ripped out.

"No, you don't need to do that," Ben said. "It really ain't no biggie. I'll bring over my pulley and I can pull the wall back in until it's straight. We can hold it there while we fix it." He looked at the wall and then around the room. "Let's see," he said. He put his hand on the center stud, which was attached to the ridge of the front porch roof. "I can put the chain around this. Now I just need something that's strong enough for me to pull on." He looked across the room. His eyes lighted on the exposed chimney that rose up through the room from the fireplace on the first floor. "I can get the other end around that chimney and pull from that. Yeah, that'll be easy."

Ben looked up and down the faulty wall. "We could put us a post right here and nail it down to the floor and up at the roof ridge," he said. "Then we could nail these two-by-fours and the porch roof to it, too. That ought keep it in place."

An easy answer, I thought. But then Ben looked up and down the wall again. "Naw," he said. "That's not going to work. You're not going to have enough strength in a post to hold that wall in place. It'll pull that post right out with it." He looked around the room again, with his eyes returning to the chimney. "Ah ha." Ben said. "I see it now. I see what I'm going to do. This chimney is going to be my anchor. I'll build a wall from here to the front wall. But this won't really be a wall. It'll be more like a divider for the room. There'll be a large opening for going back and forth. But it'll be strong enough to attach the front wall to it and hold it in place. Yes, sir. That's exactly what I'm going to do."

He had started doing it by the time I made my next trip to the farm. Ben wasn't around, but when I went upstairs I found he had rigged his pulley just as he said he would. There was a lever on the pulley system that ratcheted the chain as tight as needed. When I sighted along the wall as I had when Ben first showed the problem to me, the line was as straight as an arrow. Problem solved.

Ben had averted a catastrophe, as far as I was concerned. Who could say how unstable the wall actually was by the time he noticed it? Those tongue and groove boards I so eagerly ripped down—the ones Dan Curl said he would leave alone because they added to the structural soundness of the house—might have been a thin but essential element of a house of cards. Removing the boards probably accelerated the glacial pace of collapse that wall had begun the day it was built.

Ben's builder's eye left me grateful and impressed again. But resentment also crept in. I felt foolish for not noticing a major problem that had jumped out at Ben. And, like most of his other contributions, his solution to the problem forced a change in my plans. The front room upstairs was supposed to be the largest open space in the house. It would be a combination of children's room and dormitory. When my family had the house to ourselves, the boys would hang out and sleep there. If another family was visiting at the same time, the room would be turned over to them, with enough bunk beds for their children already there. I even thought of installing a kitchenette in one of the corners, so the visitors could make coffee or tea and prepare snacks without trumping up and down the stairs.

Ben's bracing partition forced alteration of those plans. One large, airy room would be divided into two small areas. The options for placing beds and other large furniture would be more limited. It simply wouldn't be the room I first envisioned.

Ted Watkins was right. Ben did know a lot. And I knew so little. The two of us were engaged in a struggle for control over what the house would become—a struggle so subtle, in fact, that I'm sure Ben had no idea that the battle had been joined. In that struggle, knowledge was power.

+⟞= ⟝=+

There are two major faiths in the worship of old houses. One is the Church of Preservation; the other is the Church of Renovation. They relate to each other the way Orthodox Judaism and Reform Judaism do, respectively. The Preservationists would consider my approach to the farmhouse nothing less than heresy. The Renovators would probably see me as a member of the congregation who has gone astray. If I were forced to chose between the Church of Renovation and the Church of Preservation, I'd probably declare myself a Unitarian.

The Preservationists believe in honoring the old ways. In fact, the fundamentalists among them are downright fanatical about it. They are the ones who believe an old house should be kept as old as it was the day it was new. In other words, a house constructed without indoor plumbing, electricity or (gasp) cable television should not have anything like those luxuries. After all, if God wanted houses to have that stuff, He would have built them that way. The most pious Preservationists are particularly protective of old houses of humble origin. They believe if you can't pay for ripping out all added conveniences and upgrades to make an old house look as if dirt-poor people live there, you can't afford to buy it.

The Renovators are a much less dogmatic bunch. They believe in keeping the spirit of the house, but making as many changes as it takes to make it comfortable by modern standards. Rewiring, including phone jacks, cable TV connections and computer hookups? No problem. Replumbing, including the pipes for the washing machine and dishwasher, not to mention the hot tub on the new deck? Go right ahead. The true believers in the Church of Renovation tithe generously. Their donations are tossed into a collection plate as big as a house. Everyone else calls it a "money pit."

I wasn't guided by the gospel of either of these churches when I started working on the farmhouse. I had vague and, at times, conflicting goals in mind. I wanted the house to be a living monument to what it had been. I wanted it to be the successor to the house built for my grandparents, far grander than the original. Remembering what the house was like when I was a child delighted me. So did imagining the bold changes I could make to turn its faults into virtues.

That tin roof, for example. Remembrance of the rattle of rain on that roof made me want to do whatever was possible to keep it. But the way the house was built provided very little headroom upstairs. The ceiling at the center of those rooms was eight and a half feet. From the points on both sides about seven feet from the center of the rooms, however, the ceiling slanted down rapidly, until it was only five and a half feet high at the walls. The effect was claustrophobic.

So, even as I wanted to keep the roof as it was, I devised a radical change to make those upstairs bedrooms feel more roomy. I wouldn't stop with pulling down those tongue-and-groove board ceilings, I also would remove the overhead joists. I planned to place exposed beams higher up between the rafters to brace them. Then, after insulation was installed, Sheetrock would be nailed to the rafters themselves to create the new, vaulted ceiling. Way cool, right?

Yeah, and way out of the question. This renovation innovation would be time-consuming, expensive, and impractical. The rafters already sagged. Replacing the joists with beams any higher up risked more sagging. And while the new ceilings might make the rooms feel roomier, in reality they wouldn't be one bit larger. There would be no new usable space, unless I planned to bring in potted palm trees. Anyway, my insulated ceiling would have muffled the sound of rain on the roof, the very sound that made me want to keep the tin in the first place.

I had other grandiose plans that came to naught. They all were based on "improving" something I remembered about the farm. In each case, I could not overcome the inertia that sets in with time. The farmhouse and the land knew what they had been, and what they didn't want to be.

Memories of the well made me want to bring water back to the front yard. When I was a child, I watched the well with fascination, listened to the rattle of its chain wrapping and unwrapping on the windlass, the squeak of its pulley wheel. It was a simple machine that worked. But it required human power, and not just a little of it. My grandfather could crank up a bucket full of water with one hand. While he did it his arm became sinewy and veined. Grandma had to use two hands, but she had no trouble doing it enough times in a row to fill up the black wash pot that sat over a fire in the backyard, waiting for the water, the clothes, and the pot-ash soap Grandma stirred with a stick. I don't know how old I was when I was big enough to haul up a bucket of water from the well. Five gallons of water on the end of twenty feet of chain is very heavy, even with the help of a pulley. But I do remember that when I wasn't really strong enough to pull up the water, just for fun I would lower the bucket and let it fill up just a little. I cranked the handle attached to the log the chain wrapped around as the bucket rose. Then, when the bucket was near the top, I let the handle go and stepped away. The handle spun so fast it became a blur as the bucket plummeted like a ship's anchor. I thought it was an awesome sight. Grandma caught me at it one day and had one thing to say: "Stop that child! That thing will knock your head clean off!"

The well wasn't the most reliable source of water. A really bad drought could dry it up. Plus, you never knew what you were going to pull up with the water. Mosquito larva were common in the summer. I remember a catfish once. And once there was a dead squirrel, which meant we couldn't drink water from the well for a while. As a result, I don't think sentimentality made my grandparents hesitate for a moment in the late 1960s when they decided it was time for indoor plumbing. Another well was dug around back, this time for a pump that would pull the water up and send it into the house. The well wasn't open to foreign objects, animals, or other things that might fall in and contaminate the water, and it made life easier for my grandparents.

But I had the luxury of sentimentality when my brother and I bought the farm. The house was on the city water line, so I didn't have to worry about a functioning well. I could go for a "representation" of a well. That's what I had in mind.

A mound of dirt covered what had been the well opening. I
didn't know if the well was filled in or if the opening had been
covered by a metal plate or concrete slab before dirt was piled on.
I thought about digging a trench and running pipes to the center
of the mound, most of which would be shoveled away. The pipes
would feed a fountain. I would use field stones to build a wall
around the whole thing and create a goldfish pool. Wooden
beams would form the arch over this "well," with the rest of the
accouterments for the final effect. I imagined my sons looking
over the lip of the well and tossing coins in to make a wish.

But this wishing well was worse than wishful thinking. It was
ridiculous. Why create a well that was not a well? Even with an
abundant and reliable source of water from the county system this
would be a waste of water. Grandma never wasted water. She
carried a bucket and a dipper as she went watering her many
flowers and bushes. Dipping water from the bucket, she gave
each individual plant the water it needed to thrive, nothing more.
Her frugality put my extravagant use of water to shame.

I had other ambitious plans that fell by the wayside. I wanted
to build a balcony above the front porch, with its roof supported
by four white columns. French doors would open onto it from
the front bedroom upstairs. It would be a place to take the night
air, perhaps while sipping a mint julep.

Mint julep?! The moment that thought popped into my head I
knew I wasn't looking forward to taking the night air. I was simply taking on airs. My columned balcony would have transformed
the front of the house into a tacky imitation of Tara. Again, it was
something that would take a lot of time, a lot of money, and wind
up not being very practical. During the prime time for sitting outside at night, the balcony would be a mosquito feeding ground.

Then there was the garage-workshop with a glass-walled studio on top. That was going to be built around in the back on the
spot where my grandparents' old storage shed had stood. I had
spent many hours in that shed as a child, looking at all the tools
and odds and ends stashed away there. The best thing to do was
to climb up into the loft. That was where Grandma put away all

the books and magazines she had read and reread until they weren't worth reading any more. While I might thumb through the books, I devoured the magazines. There were *Life*, *Look* and *National Geographic*. There was *Jet*, the African-American weekly news magazine. I specifically remember coming across the issue that featured the murder of Emmit Till, who had been accused of trying to sweet-talk to a white girl and wound up wrapped in chains at the bottom of a river in Mississippi. *Jet* was known for its gory photographs. This one had a picture of Till's bloated body in the casket at his funeral in Chicago, the city he had left to spend the summer with relatives in Mississippi, apparently unaware of some of the state's strictly enforced social mores.

That loft also was where Grandma kept what she called "old stuff"—as in "Child, leave that old stuff alone." Today, it would be called "expensive stuff"—as in antiques. They were mostly gadgets that either didn't work or weren't of use any more. My favorite was a stereoscope. Because it had two thick lenses I guessed it was used to look at something. I figured out it was for pictures, but I never found any of the pairs that were specially made so the device merged them into one image that appeared three-dimensional.

The studio I had in mind would be a writing room, as well as a place to enjoy books and magazine and old stuff. Its height would allow a view down into the small valley where the creek ran, and across the hills at the setting sun.

But building the garage-workshop-studio would be like building another house. It would require permits and inspections. Trenches would have to be dug and water and sewer pipes laid. The place would have to be wired. I considered the time and expense and decided, "No, not yet. Maybe later."

Why did I veer off into these flights of fancy when I had enough work to do just making the farmhouse livable? At first, I told myself I was inspired by some part of the house whose spirit I wanted to keep alive. The balcony would have re-created the old front porch, the one with wood floors instead of a concrete slab. The wishing well fountain obviously evoked the original well. The garage-workshop-studio derived from the old storage shed and its loft.

But I wasn't planning to re-create those favorite features. I was planning to best them with something more elaborate and even more to my liking than the original. I once heard a radio show about the mind, including a discussion of memory. An expert in the field said the way our brain remembers isn't the way most people think it does. They see a filing system of cabinets for things that happened to us and things we need to know. That's too static a concept of memory, the expert said. The brain doesn't just file something away and then find it in the proper folder when needed. The brain constantly goes back to our memories and retrieves them, whether we need them or even realize their file is being opened. What the brain does is continually "improve" our memories. And by "improve," the expert didn't mean make them sharper or more precise or more complete. He meant the brain makes the memories more like we want them to be. As time goes by, whether experiences were good or bad, we remember them more like we think they should have happened. If we want to remember ourselves as being more heroic in a certain situation, that's the direction our memory moves. If we want to remember ourselves as victimized, the brain sends memory down that lane.

Taken another way, the mind is a film editor working with miles and miles of raw footage. Any section of film contains a movie—a memory, if you will. But each movie can be manipulated by the mind-as-film-editor. What happens in a movie depends on camera angles, the sequence in which events are presented, what's left on the cutting-room floor, and other factors the film editor controls. He can even take footage from completely unrelated sections and splice it into his movie. Orson Welles, among the greatest movie makers, was forever re-editing his films. So, too, is the human mind.

So perhaps my grand remodeling plans were manifestations of this theory of memory. What I remember of those elements of the farm had evolved into what I wanted them to be. I was

simply trying to carry the process to conclusion, when there
before me would be the well, the porch, the shed—exactly as
I wish they had been.

⊹⊱ ⊰⊹

Ben advised me not to do any major work on the house until the
job of stabilizing the wall had been finished. That might take a
few weeks, because his schedule included a trip and some other
work that would keep him away from the farmhouse most of the
time. That required delaying the next big step in the renovation—putting on new siding.

Ted Watkins and I had nailed and stapled huge sheets of plastic to the house, completely wrapping it. I called our creation
"Christo Comes to Butts County." There was nothing artistic
about it, of course. The plastic was literally a stop-gap measure—
something to stop the winter wind from coming in through the
many gaps in the damaged and warped wood siding. The new
siding would make the house more or less weather-tight, which,
as Ben pointed out, was the first thing I should have done when
I started the renovation.

After risking my neck on unstable scaffolding to tear down the
old vinyl siding—most of the time alone, but sometimes with
Ted's help—I had decided to replace it with new vinyl siding. For
such a sin I no doubt would be excommunicated, if not cast
directly into hell, by the Church of Preservation. The Church of
Renovation would only require an act of penitence, perhaps by
including in the remodeling a "country kitchen" so filled with
modern cooking conveniences that my grandmother wouldn't
know how to begin baking a batch of biscuits there.

Replacing the vinyl instead of trying to replicate the original
wood siding was not an easy decision. Whoever sold the siding to
my grandmother really took advantage of her. They did a lousy
job. They intended to cover up cosmetic problems. But, as I
explained earlier, their work created serious structural problems

by promoting extensive water rot. The siding was far from weather-tight. It allowed water to seep in and then held it there. If I had wanted to stick with wood, I estimated that more than half the siding would have to be replaced, along with replacing rotted studs with new ones so there would be something solid to nail the boards to.

That would be an endless job, tantamount to tearing down the whole house and rebuilding it. The original lap siding boards would have to be matched. Then there would be a substantial painting job. And that raised another small problem that had me stumped.

If going back to wood siding was for authenticity's sake, it only made sense to be as authentic as possible. That meant going back to the original color of the house. The problem was that there was disagreement about what that color was.

I talked to aunts and uncles, brothers and cousins—people who had either lived in or regularly visited the farm for most of their lives—and no consensus emerged about what color, or colors, the house had been.

My mother said she thought it was yellow at one point, and then gray. One of my brothers said it had always been white, like the vinyl siding. An uncle remembered a light blue. What was my memory of the color? If forced to swear about it, I would be as truthful as a witness hauled before a congressional committee. "I have no specific recollection of any of that," I would say. Most of my memories of the house come back to me in the most vivid details, but I really can't remember a color for the house. A man who can't remember the color of the eyes of the woman he loves, I can understand. But not being able to recall the color of the ancestral home? Ridiculous!

I hoped some old pictures Mom dug out would solve the mystery, but they didn't. The only color snapshots were taken after the siding had been put up. The vintage photos, including some taken when the house was brand new, were in black and white. Most of those pictures were of people standing in front of a car parked in the driveway to the farm. The few that were taken of people standing beside the house gave no clue about color. In fact, some of the pictures make the house look as if the siding was just bare, unpainted and unprotected from the weather. That old black-and-white camera didn't scratch the surface on the color question, so I did some scratching of my own. Where water couldn't get in, the old vinyl siding had preserved what was underneath. The front porch was one such place. The wood siding there was painted the same reddish-brown color as the rest of the house. I gently scraped the paint, working my way back to the first coating. As far as I could tell, the first coat was the last coat. But that seemed the most unlikely answer I could have found. It meant the house had been painted only once, and that the paint job had held up for almost sixty years. If that was true, they sure don't make paint the way they used to.

I had one more place to look for an answer. Some of the wood siding that still was in good shape had been sawed away when I enlarged windows or created new openings. I looked at the cross sections of pieces of those siding boards. Again, there was only one coat of paint evident. Perhaps this was one of those rare cases in which the unlikeliest answer is the correct one.

In the end, identifying the original color of the house would not have made a difference. I decided that having new vinyl siding installed had to win out over sentiment. It would require only that the house be structurally sound, not virtually rebuilt. Once the house was ready to have the vinyl siding put up, it could be done quickly, taking no more than four or five days. (That's four or five days in real time, not Austin and A. T. time.) And the house would never have to be painted again.

So the finished farmhouse would have vinyl siding. I know that's an anomaly that even restoration agnostics would look upon with disdain. But I kept the faith as best I could. Who knows? Perhaps my sons will do better some day. Years from now, when they have lots of money and lots of time, maybe they'll rip down the tacky vinyl siding Dad settled on, not as a result of bad taste, but in a moment of weakness. They will scour lumber yards to find an exact match for the old lap siding. They will commission a chemical analysis to determine the original paint and its color. They will atone for the sins of their father. They may even earn dispensation from the Church of Preservation. Miracles do happen, don't they?

CHAPTER 9

It was mid-March, but the wind blew as if April had already arrived. It rushed through the top of the Georgia pine on the north side of the farmhouse, set the pine needles vibrating like wind instruments' reeds, and made the tree sing and take its bows. It was not weather for working in high places. But there went sixty-three-year-old Ben Hamilton, not only walking in the wind across the steeply pitched roof, but carrying a four-by-eight-foot sheet of plywood while doing it.

He might as well have been walking on water, as far as I was concerned. That's how far beyond my understanding the feat was. He walked on the roof's plywood decking; there were no rough-textured shingles to grip the soles of his shoes. The smooth surface was slippery to begin with, and most of the pieces had been sawed, coating them with a sawdust film that made them ten times more slippery. And each plywood sheet Ben carried might as well have been a sail. It caught the wind, which pushed and pulled him as he walked. A sudden gust could throw Ben off balance and send him rolling down the roof and over the edge to a twenty-five-foot fall to the ground.

While Ben did this dangerous work, I stood safely on the

platform he had built on top of the front porch roof. My job was to get the sheets of plywood from the ground up to that platform, saw them, if necessary, and hand them to Ben. He then carried them to the spot where he laid them across the exposed rafters and nailed them in place. We were in the early stages of replacing the tin roof with a shingled one. Even as the work progressed, I had second thoughts.

I had tried everything I could think of to keep a metal roof over the house. Ted Watkins and I spent a lot of time up there patching the rusted tin. Ted walked confidently across the roof carrying a can of roofing cement. I moved ever so slowly, either crawling on my hands and knees or sliding my butt along the tin to reduce the chances of falling to as close to zero as I could get. There were a few places where the tin had rusted all the way through and formed small holes. But mostly we dabbed the black roofing cement where the old roofing nails had worked their way loose or where the lead heads of the nails, which had spread out and snugly covered the nail hole when they were driven home, had deteriorated and fallen off. This method didn't add to the beauty of the roof (as if it had any to add to), but it would keep the rain from dripping in for a while.

I also checked into various coatings that could be applied to the roof. These were supposed to both plug the leaks and make the roof look better. I called two roof-coating companies. I thought it was significant that both salesmen I talked to presumed I was talking about something other than an actual house. One man returned a voice mail message I left for him: "Mr. Head, I'm returning your call about that chicken house roof you're working on down in Butts County." The other said in the middle of our conversation, "Now, how big is this barn roof you're talking about?"

These men were used to helping farmers get a few more years out of tin roofs on chicken houses and barns, not houses. But once I told them I was trying to salvage the rusted tin roof on a farm house, they assured me that their coatings would make it as good as new. The coatings would stop rust, stop leaks and last ten to twenty years. It sounded too good to be true, which probably meant it was too good to be true. But I wanted to find out more. I tried to make appointments for someone from the companies to come down and take a look at the roof and explain exactly how their products would work. It was difficult to find anyone willing to come all the way to Jackson from the suburbs north of Atlanta where the companies were located.

I was surprised one day, though, while I was working high up on scaffolding at the back of the house. I heard someone calling. When I looked down there was a man looking up. I climbed down. He introduced himself as a representative of one of the roof-coating companies. Then he looked the house up and down and said, "Are you doing all this by yourself?"

"Pretty much," I said.

"You renovating it to sell it?"

"No. This was my grandparents' farm. My brother and I bought it to keep it in the family. I'm trying to do as much of the work restoring the house myself as I can. I've had a couple of contractors do some work, but the rest I'm doing myself."

"Well, this is really something," he said. "This is just a good thing to do. I wanted to do the same thing when my grandparents died. It was just a little old house on some land out in the country, but I wanted to get out there and fix it up. But I never made the time to do it. We just let it go."

He stepped back and looked up. "So what are you planning to do about the roof?" he asked.

"I'd like to save it if I can. It's pretty rusty, and there are some leaks, but most of it seems to be sound. Mostly, what it needs is cosmetic."

"Our system can stop the leaks and improve the look, too. We put patches over all the nails and any holes. A primer goes over that, and then the coating. Have you thought about what color you would want?"

"I've thought about red," I said, "but I'm afraid that might be a bit much."

"It's just a matter of what your preference is." He walked away from the house, into the tall grass on the northern side. He looked up at the roof from that vantage point. "The main problem is the rust," he said. "We'd need to get as much of that off as possible. Pressure washing might do that."

"Is this something I can do myself?"

"You can," he said. "But I wouldn't recommend it. It's a big job." He was quiet for a moment. "I'll tell you what," he said. "I really like what you're doing here. I'm going to try to get the company to give you the coating. And I think I can get a crew to come down and put it on for you. I wouldn't charge for anything except the labor. I know they'll do a good job."

"That would be great."

"Let me talk to my boss and see if he'll agree to it. I think he will. I'd really like to help you out with this in some way. I'll give you a call as soon as I know something."

I thanked him. We shook hands. I never heard from him again.

So I was left with little choice but to tear off the tin. Ben and I could do much of the work from inside, standing on stepladders and knocking the sheets of tin up and away from the rafters. The work was a lot tougher where the metal was sound and the nails still firmly embedded in the hard wood. In other places the tin was partially rusted and soft. It would tear away from the rafter, leaving a hole like a gunshot wound. And in some cases the nails had been so loosened by the movement of the rafters or the tin's expansion and contraction in the heat and the cold that they could be pulled out by hand. Removing the only roof the farmhouse had had for almost sixty years took about a day's work between the two of us.

Even at that point, I couldn't let go of the idea of having a metal roof. My family took a spring-break trip down to St. George Island on Florida's Gulf Coast. Most of the houses there had metal roofs, but not the shiny tin my grandparents would recognize. These roofs came in a rainbow of colors—white, blues, greens, reds, browns. They were beautiful. I pictured one on the farmhouse. It would be a good fit. Ben was right that the dressed-up house needed a new hat. Those Gulf Coast houses showed me I could have both the new hat—and a fashionable one, at that—and the old-time sound of rain rattling on the tin.

But it was too late. Ben had already started laying down the plywood decking for the shingle roof. Maybe in twenty years or so, when the shingles are faded and brittle, I can get that new metal roof. That will be a colorful hat the house can wear for another sixty years.

━━ ━━

The wood used to build the house probably didn't have to travel very far from the place where the trees were felled to the place where the lumber was nailed. Much of Middle Georgia was still covered with what seemed an inexhaustible supply of pine trees. We called the men who harvested the forests pulpwooders, even if the trees they cut down weren't headed to mills to be reduced to pulp and made into paper. The roar of their saws echoed through the woods. The long logs shorn of their limbs were stacked as high as possible on open-bed trucks. It was the leavings of these men that I helped Grandpa scavenge so he could cut it up and sell it as firewood.

The loaded pulpwood trucks were so weighed down with pine logs that you would have thought their tires would flatten. It seemed half the length of the logs extended beyond the end of the truck bed, held precariously in place by chains that seemed too thin for the job. When the pulpwood trucks emerged from the woods and rumbled onto the highways, other drivers kept their distance. Driving behind one felt like standing under the Sword of Damocles. The truck's load always seemed on the verge of breaking loose and flying off the trucks like gigantic spears. Drivers craned their necks and eased into the passing lane to check for oncoming traffic before speeding past the truck, putting as much distance between themselves and danger as possible.

I suspect they were still harvesting old growth trees in Butts County when the farmhouse was built in 1940. The house's studs, joists, and headers were made of wood much darker and denser than the stuff you find in lumberyards today. And it wasn't just the

aging of the old wood. When I cut it or drilled into it, the wood
at its core was still harder than the wood I am used to. Cross-cuts
of the old lumber showed a light brown that darkened to a red-
dish color. The darkest wood seemed as hard as steel.

When the house was built, Butts County was dotted with
mom-and-pop sawmills. (Actually, they would've been pop-and-
sons, of course.) Most of them were set up in the woods, right
where the trees were being cut down. They had to keep things
simple. Their lumber was rough-cut. Saws were set so that if they
were producing two-by-four studs, the studs were as close as they
could get to two inches thick and four inches wide. Of course,
some were more precise in their settings than others. In fact,
everyone tended to be off by at least a little bit. And, in terms of
aesthetics, rough-cut wood looked, well, rough.

Eventually, standards for the dimensions of lumber were set
throughout the industry, whether the producers were large companies or family-run operations. This involved "dressing" the
lumber—planing it down to the accepted thickness and width.
Planing—shaving down the wood thin layer by thin layer—was
more precise than rough cutting. And it produced smooth surfaces that looked better. One of the results of this improvement,
however, is that lumber shrank from its "true" size. A two-by-
four is actually one and a half inches thick and three and a half
inches wide. Some might consider this an exercise in downsizing
to pump up profits (sort of like the Baby Ruth candy bar, which
went from meal-size when I was a kid, to today's more expensive
bite-sized bar). But the industry really had no practical alternative.
There had to be a margin of error that was larger than the desired
end result in order for everyone to plane down to the standard.
The small saw mills out in the Butts County woods sold their
lumber to a big saw mill in town. Once there, the lumber was
dressed—planed to the prescribed sizes.

The move to industrywide standards created a demarcation in
house building. There was a point at which the era of houses built
with rough-cut lumber was followed by the era of dressed lumber, the era in which we still live. There was a transition period,

of course, when less and less rough-cut lumber was used as more and more dressed lumber was used. But, in general, houses should have been built with one grade of lumber or the other.

That presented a puzzle for me as I worked on the farmhouse. I kept running into structural timber that didn't seem to fit. Some studs might be more narrow than the footing they rested on. The dimensions of headers varied. And some boards—especially the rafters—had rough-cut surfaces.

What was going on? It was as if the house builders bounced back and forth between the rough-cut and dressed lumber eras. But I thought that was unlikely. This was just another mystery the house mischievously put before me, saying, "Solve it if you can."

⊢━ ━⊣

Ben had started decking the roof working alone. He built an ingenious contraption to accomplish the difficult job of getting the plywood from the ground to the roof. It consisted of a holder for the sheets that resembled a pair of stilts made of two-by-fours rising from the ground and leaning against the platform on top of the porch roof. A short piece of two-by-six board was nailed about halfway up the inside of each two-by-four, where the footrests for stilts would have been. Plywood sheets were stacked on the top of the portion of the two-by-six that protruded beyond the edges of the two-by-fours. Then Ben could climb a ladder to the platform, reach down and grab the edge of a plywood sheet and slide it the rest of the way up.

I stood admiring Ben's handiwork after I arrived at the farm that Saturday morning in mid-March. He called to me from the rooftop. "So there you are," he said. "Are you ready to go to work?"

It was a little before 9:00 A.M. "Sure," I said. "What do you want me to do?"

"You can bring plywood from that pile over yonder and put it here," he said, pointing to the two-by-four stilts. "Wait a minute. I'll come down and show you how to do it."

I think I know how to pick up a piece of plywood and carry it, I thought. Ben must have read my mind. When we got to the plywood pile, he said, "Let's see how you're going to pick it up."

I moved around so I was at the middle of the sheets length-wise. I reached for the far edge. I had a hard time lifting it, and when I finally managed to, the sheet began sliding off the stack. I had to bend down to catch it. Lifting the plywood from there was difficult, not so much because it was heavy, but because it was awkward to handle.

"Let me show you how to do it," Ben said. He lifted a corner of a sheet with one hand and pulled it around until the plywood was crossways to the stack. He pulled the plywood until half of it was off the stack. With the sheet balanced, he walked to its middle, put one hand on the top and the other on the bottom, bent his knees and lifted the plywood flat against his shoulder. "It's all a matter of leverage and balance," he said. "What did the man say? That if he had a lever big enough he could move the earth."

I was only concerned about moving plywood. Following Ben's instructions, I managed to get a sheet on my shoulder and walk with it over to Ben's lift device. I turned the sheet and had a tough time getting it onto the "stilts."

"Let me show you," Ben said. He took the plywood from me. Just as I did, Ben turned the sheet so it could be stood up. But instead of trying to lift it all the way, he leaned the top against the two-by-fours. Then he turned to me. "Now, this is important," he said. "Watch the way I get this up there." His hands were cupped underneath the sheet's bottom edge. He started lifting it up. When the bottom of the sheet was about shoulder high, he turned his hands around. That way, he pushed the plywood up instead of continuing to lift it. "If you do it this way, it's not going to come back down on you," Ben said.

So . . . I was assigned to manual labor while Ben handled the craftsmanship. As I stacked the plywood sheets, he would lift them, saw them to the needed size, and then take them onto the roof and nail them to the rafters. Ben soon decided this wasn't the most efficient way to do things. Both of us were spending most of our time going back and forth instead of actually working on the roof.

"I'll tell you what," he said. "You stack up five or six more sheets and then come up here. We're going to do something different."

After I climbed up on the platform, Ben told me the new plan. I would lift the sheets up and cut them to lengths he called out to me. He would spend all of his time on the roof, measuring, putting the plywood in place, and nailing it down. He showed me how to pull the plywood up using my legs instead of straining my back. He showed me how to get the plywood onto the two sawhorses with a spin move that looked like a ballet step or the pivot by a second baseman on a double play. And he showed me how to use a drywall T-square to make the pencil mark for my cut across the plywood.

I was nervous as I pushed the power saw for the long cuts across the plywood. This was something I just wasn't good at. I knew it from all the times I had sawed through studs or boards and found that the cuts weren't straight. It didn't make a big difference in most of those cases, but I knew it mattered with the plywood. The pieces had to fit snugly. Gaps would invite leaks, even with the tarpaper and shingles on top. In addition, I could feel Ben's eyes on me every time he had to wait for me to get the next piece he needed. The object of this division of labor, after all, was to allow him to keep going on the time-consuming part of the job while I did the things that could be done quickly. There were times when Ben's impatience was palpable. I responded by trying to speed up everything I was doing. And when I did that, I dropped the plywood a few times and mismeasured a piece.

"When you get in a hurry, you get a lot less done," Ben finally said. I didn't say anything. I just tried to calm down and slow down. I doubled-checked every measurement. I crept along the cut line with the power saw in an effort to keep it straight. The blade still wavered back and forth along the line like a drunk taking a roadside sobriety test.

"You're making these cuts crooked," Ben said. "Every time you do, you're messing up my straight lines on the decking."

I tried to be super careful on the next cut. After Ben carried it over and laid it in place, he called to me. "John," he said. "Look at this. Look at how far off this piece is."

As the Bard might say, I had made the unstraightest cut of all. It was so crooked that when Ben laid it down there were gaps between it and the pieces beside it and below it. "You're going to have to cut another piece," Ben said.

He watched over me. I tried to move the saw an inch at a time, figuring I could surely cut straight in small increments. It didn't work. The saw acted as if it just didn't want to follow the line.

"You know why you're making so many mistakes?" Ben asked.

"No," I said, trying to keep exasperation out of my voice. "I don't."

"You're making mistakes because you're trying to be too careful," he said. "If you saw too slow you'll never cut it straight."

I was beginning to feel like a novice in a Buddhist monastery. Ben was the Zen master, and any minute he would say it would be time for me to go into the world when I could snatch a pebble from his hand.

"Let me have the saw," he said as he jumped down from the roof onto the platform.

He took the tool in his left hand and started it before putting it close to the edge of the plywood. Then he cut quickly along the line, with nary a waver. "You have to do it like you have some confidence," Ben said. "You can't let the saw think you're afraid."

Can't let the saw think I'm afraid? I thought. Can we let the saw think anything? This really was a lesson in the Zen of carpentry.

"Now, being left-handed, I've got an advantage over you," Ben said. "I can see straight into the window of the cut—see where the blade is going. You have to sort of lean over to do that. But you still should be able to make a straight cut."

I tried again, this time attempting to summon up some pseudo-confidence. I held my breath as Ben took the piece and put it down. "That's better," he said. "It's not 100 percent straight, but it's good enough."

I went on sawing. I felt I was doing better, but I knew the cuts were at least a little off. Ben said nothing, which I took as a good sign. Then he called to me again. "John, come over here and look at this."

Uh, oh. I walked to the edge of the roof and looked at the piece of plywood Ben had just put down. I didn't see any large gaps. Couldn't see any gaps at all. I wondered what was wrong.

"This one is just about perfect," Ben said. "Cut as straight as can be. Now that's what I'm talking about."

"Must have happened by accident," I said.

"No, no," Ben said. "I was noticing you were getting better with each cut. We'll make a carpenter out of you yet."

I felt elated, a moment of pure joy. I started cutting with confidence. I was the saw and the saw was me. We became one. Zen mastery of wood-cutting at last.

We worked steadily, but the light was fading. Just a few more pieces had to be placed around the chimney and the decking would be done. Ben wanted to finish before dark and not have to worry about coming back Sunday. The forecast was for a chance of rain, and for a greater chance by Monday. Ben didn't want to leave any of the roof open.

Making the pieces fit tightly around the chimney took careful measurements and precise cutting. Even with my newfound confidence, I couldn't do this work fast enough to suit Ben. He grew more impatient as it got darker. "I think I better do these," he told me. "We haven't got much time."

He made the measurements and marked the plywood for the cuts. He was more than twice as fast as I was. Three more pieces had to be placed around the chimney. The first two fit perfectly. Then came the last one. It didn't fit. It was off. By a lot.

"What the hell happened here?" Ben said. He studied it for a few moments. "Oh, I see," he said. "I measured wrong. I got in a hurry and did it wrong. I should have known better. We'll fix that up right quick."

I was stunned that Ben had made a mistake; making mistakes was my job, after all.

Ben set things straight quickly. We both climbed down from the platform. Ben said he was tired and hungry. He was going to get home right away. I told him I would clean up. I walked with him to where his van was parked in the driveway. Ben turned around and looked up at the roof. "Now don't that look a lot better already?" he asked. "Aren't you glad you didn't keep that rusty old roof after you're going to put so much into fixing up the house?"

"It does look good," I said, refusing to speak ill of the dearly departed tin roof.

"Well, if it gets some rain on it, it's not going to hurt it," Ben said. "It'll dry out. We'll put the drips and flashing on next week and we'll be ready for the roofer to come in and do the shingles."

I wanted to tell Ben how much what he was doing meant to me. I didn't know if I could. I didn't know if he'd want to hear it.

"Ben," I began. "I really appreciate all the help you've given me. I would have been completely lost if it weren't for you."

"Don't worry about it, John," Ben said. "I said I would stick with you until you got to where you could go the rest of the way on your own, and I will."

We shook hands and said we'd see each other the following week. I could tell Ben was bone tired. He moved slowly, and a weariness seemed to pull at him as he climbed into his van. He backed up, turned around, and pulled out onto the highway. I waved as he headed toward home. He gave a small wave back.

It was dark by the time I had gathered the tools and stacked scraps of plywood and lumber. I was tired myself. I sat on the edge of the front porch to rest for a few minutes. The concrete was cold, but I didn't mind.

Sitting there, I thought about what it was like working with Ben. He was teaching me a lot without even trying. He taught me things even when I resisted learning. He could be cutting and comforting in the things he said. I envied him and feared him. I cringed before his rebukes and was swelled with pride by his praise. I wanted to do things my way and I wanted to do things in ways that would please him. I resented it when he demanded perfection from me and I fully expected perfection from him.

I sat there alone in the darkness and the cold and thought all those things. And then the combined weight of all those thoughts squeezed one more notion out of me.

So this is what it's like to have a father.

CHAPTER 10

I made my last stand for the solarium. One more time, I tried to save that wonder of structural engineering ingenuity I wanted to build where the farmhouse's back porch had been. I wanted to create that illusion of a room defying gravity, floating on air. The glass walls on three sides would give a panoramic view of the countryside equivalent to looking at the earth from an orbiting spaceship. Call it pride of architectureship or just plain stubbornness, I wanted to build that room, and I wanted to build it exactly as I had conceived it.

I had made strategic retreats in this battle with Ben Hamilton in order to survive and fight again another day. In the beginning it was a dining room. The cinderblock foundation of the old back porch would stay, but I installed new sills and floor joists. My innovation would be using those two-by-twelve boards to extend the floor almost a foot beyond the foundation. This was not only for aesthetics. Its practical purpose was to create more space. The enlarged room would be about nine feet by twelve feet. And those glass walls would give the room a more spacious feel.

I was quite pleased with myself until Ben brought my design up short—literally. "Your dimensions are still too small," he said. "Once you get a table and chairs in there you're not going to have hardly enough room to turn around."

He was right, of course. Even a small table with four chairs would fill up the room. Anyone who pulled their chair away from the table would risk crashing through one of those glass walls. The dining room would feel more like a dining closet.

So I stopped calling it a dining room. It became a breakfast nook. The word "nook" carried the connotation of intentional closeness. This room definitely would fit that bill. Still too small, Ben said. There wasn't enough room for four people to eat, even if they sat in folding chairs and balanced their cereal bowls on their laps. The name change meant I could say the room was large for a nook. That didn't make it any larger, though.

Finally, I called the room a solarium. There would be no need for a table. No need to worry about having enough space to sit down and eat. This would be a place to sit to feel the warmth of the sun and enjoy the view. Never mind that the warmth of the Georgia sun passing through all that glass in July would turn the room into a solar oven where molten vinyl chairs would stick to people's butts when they tried to stand up. And never mind that the only view from the back of the house for the next few years would be of acres of kudzu. I could accept such minor drawbacks in exchange for the illusion of a room floating on air.

Ben probably knew at that point that he was not dealing with a rational being. So he dropped any discussion of the dining room/breakfast nook/solarium while we worked on the roof. We were like Russian and American allies who knew we were bound to be adversaries once our common enemy was defeated. Finishing the roof meant moving onto to the next project. The battle was rejoined.

Ben shifted tactics. Instead of appealing to my common sense, he returned to his original assault, using the laws of physics as a weapon. If you could make a room float you would defeat gravity, Ben explained. Making a room to appear to float would only make gravity angry.

My description of the extensive bracing I planned to put under the floor extension didn't satisfy Ben. "It doesn't matter how you brace it," Ben said. "You're still going to have the walls setting right on the edge of it, and you're going to have a roof on top of that. All that weight being pulled down. Think about what that's going to do over the years. That two-by-twelve is going to curl down. Eventually you're going to lose it. It's going to happen. There's no way to keep it from happening."

Everything Ben said made sense, but I wasn't ready to give in. I felt he owed it to me to indulge my foolishness this time. I had conceded the roof to him, giving up my sentimental desire to keep the tin. It was my turn to win one.

Ben must have sensed my refusal to be bested again. Instead of arguing about why I couldn't have what I wanted, he started talking about what I could have instead.

"You know, since you're already doing the work and buying the materials, it won't take you much more time or cost you much more money to go ahead and build a larger room that you can really get some use out of," he said. "If you go ahead and build the smaller room, if you decide later on that you have to add more space, it's going to be a much more expensive job and will take much longer to do it. You do it now you can have it exactly the way you're going to want it."

Then Ben stepped off some distances, laying down pieces of wood to mark his stopping points. "You can have a room that comes out this far," he said, "and goes all the way across to there."

The room Ben put into my mind was sixteen feet by twenty feet. It would be more than three times as large as my erstwhile dining room/solarium. I imagined the possibilities. There would be space enough for a dining area with a table for eight, with more room to spare. That breakfast nook could be put in the corner close to the kitchen by having a shared countertop in the open area between the two rooms. And a family area with a couch and chairs around an entertainment center would fit into the other end of the room.

Ben knew he had me hooked. He gently reeled me in, even as he listened to my too-ambitious ideas, which, if completely realized, would make this large living area as cramped as the small space I originally wanted. "That might work," he said. "But you'll have a better idea of what you can get in there when the room is done."

I didn't even put up that much of a fight for the one feature I wanted to retain from my first design—the wall-to-wall glass. I envisioned a series of ceiling-to-floor picture windows forming the room's three exterior walls. Entrance to the room from the backyard would be through sliding glass doors.

"That's a lot of glass," Ben said in an understatement on the order of saying the Pacific Ocean is a lot of water. "It's going to take a lot of air conditioning to keep it cool in the summer and a lot of heating to keep it warm in the winter. And if you can't open the windows, how are you going to air the room out?"

I didn't have answers for Ben's objections. I told him I was trying to get as much light into the room as possible and to afford good views of the land. Some day the kudzu would be gone, and I wanted to sit in that room and look at the valley that ran down to the creek and at the hill that rose up on the other side to form the western horizon.

"You can put in double-hung windows and make them just about as big as you want," Ben suggested. "Another thing you ought to think about is whether you want a deck that you can walk out onto from this room. Do you want one in the back or one toward the front? If you have the one toward the front, you can put in glass doors that will give you another way in and let in more light. And there's nothing that says you can't put a deck on both sides."

Of course, I couldn't resist the more extravagant option. "I think two decks would be nice," I said.

"Well, I'll tell you what," Ben said. "Why don't you do a floor plan and some sketches of what you want? Put in the windows and exactly where you want them and decide exactly what size you want them to be. We can dig the trenches for the footing and get a cinderblock foundation in. Then we can frame it. It shouldn't take no time at all."

He made it sound as if we were starting a little weekend

home-repair project. Even a weekend job took me at least a week to complete. This was construction of a room from scratch. Yet Ben said we could knock it off in "no time at all." Not long ago, I wouldn't have dreamed of tackling something like this. Now I was confident we would get it done. I believed in Ben.

<hr />

"You got to have a good foundation, or you might as well not bother building it," Ben said. "That's the first thing the inspector will check, and if it isn't right he'll make you tear it up and start over again."

The county building inspector would have to come out and look at our work every step along the way, Ben told me. He was skeptical when I told him none of the work done on the house before had been inspected because the contractors said it wasn't required for repair work. "The inspector is going to catch you if you don't call him," Ben said. "If that happens, he can come out and make you redo anything that isn't right. Might as well get him here from the beginning." So I went to the courthouse and got a permit for a room addition. I dreaded what would happen if an inspector who came out to check the dining room work stepped inside and looked at the new plumbing. I had done my best to correct the problems with Bobby the Plumber's work, but I doubted I had done nearly enough to bring it up to standard.

The immediate worry, though, was getting the dining room done. Ben marked its boundaries based on the floor plan I drew for him. He drove four steel spikes into the ground. Two were next to the house and two were at what would become the far corners of the room. String that stretched from one spike to another provided the straight line along which the trenches for the foundation footing would be dug. Before we could do any digging, part of the concrete steps that had led to the back porch had to be demolished. It was in the way of the trench for the footing. Ben and I took turns pounding on the concrete with a sledgehammer.

We hadn't knocked away much concrete when we found large stones underneath. These obviously had been part of the original steps when the house was built. "They used to use fieldstones for foundations all the time," Ben said.

I remembered the support pillars of stacked stones Jim Gann found the first time he crawled under the house. I tried to picture the pillars the house rested on when I was a child. This was when the space under the house was open, before cinderblock walls closed it all around. Were those pillars made of fieldstone or bricks? And what about the well in the front yard? That, I knew, wasn't brick. It had to be made of mortared stones. I wondered where they would have found so many stones suitable for what they wanted to build.

"Do you think they brought these in from somewhere when they built the house?" I asked Ben.

He laughed. "They wouldn't need to bring them in from nowhere," he said. "When your granddaddy started working the land I doubt he could plow a row without turning up a big rock. They could have found more fieldstones than they ever would need right around here."

We went back to pounding the concrete. Sometimes it broke off in big chunks. Sometimes it refused to be broken, sending out chips that stung our faces with each blow. When I broke off one large piece, a rusted chain dangled from the concrete. Ben and I looked closer. There was more chain and some rusted metal in the concrete. "I bet you don't know what that is," Ben said.

"That's part of a singletree," I said. "It's used to hitch the mule to a plow."

"How did you know that?"

"I saw Grandpa plowing the field lots of times," I said. "One time he even let me plow a row. I remember what the harness for the mule looked like."

"That thing must be really old," Ben said.

"I found a bunch of old hand tools when I cleared away that old storage house they knocked down," I said. "I'm going to save them and display them somewhere in the house when I'm done."

We went back to work, steadily clearing the concrete and stones out of the way. And while we labored, I thought about what it must have been like for Grandpa when he bought the land and turned it into a farm. Getting those stones out of his fields must have been back-breaking work. And he probably started the job using the same kind of equipment farmers had used for a hundred years. I found a draw knife among the rusted tools in the ruins of the old shed. Grandpa could have used it to hand-shape timber into lumber or handles or other things he needed. Eventually, he had all kinds of manufactured tools and agricultural machinery he either owned or leased. But in the beginning it was hand-to-hand combat with the land.

We finished the demolition late that Saturday afternoon. Ben had some other things to do. He left it to me to start digging the trench. "You want it to be about four inches deep," he told me. "Try to keep it as level as you can. It's no problem if it's a little bit off, 'cause we can have the concrete mixed soupy and it will level itself." He looked at the string that marked the end of the room. The string stretched across ground that rose into a small hill. "We're going to have to do a step-up over there to keep it level. In other words, we'll dig down and keep it level a little ways. That's going to make the trench look like it's going deeper. When we're about four inches deeper than a course of cinderblocks, we're gong to stop that trench and start another higher up from that point and just keep digging it at least four inches deep and keep it along the string. And we'll make the trench fourteen inches wide so we'll have four inches on either side of the cinderblock."

Ben paused in thought for a moment. "This is going to be a little complicated," he said. "Maybe you better wait and let me dig the trench. I can get by here next week and do it."

"I'll get started and do as much as I can," I said. "You can finish whatever I don't get done."

"You can go ahead and get started on this part," Ben said, indicating the string marking the path for the trench that had been blocked by the steps. "Don't bother with the rest. If you never dug for footing before, you're liable to mess it up. And if you do it wrong I'll just have to do it over."

I steamed with resentment after Ben left. Did he think I was too dumb to be trusted with ditch-digging? There was nothing complicated about it. If he thought I couldn't grasp the concepts of keeping a trench level while digging in ground that went uphill, he was wrong. I would show him. I would do the job and do it so well he wouldn't have to change a thing.

First, I had to decide whether to follow Ben's instructions or change something he said that I thought was wrong. He said the trench should be about fourteen inches wide to allow for a margin of four inches on either side of the cinderblocks. But the blocks were eight inches wide. Add four inches on both sides and you had sixteen inches, not fourteen. I went with sixteen inches, figuring that making the trench wider than required was preferable to making it too narrow.

I used a mattock to start the trench at the side of the house. Just a little digging uncovered the concrete footing that had been put in for the walls enclosing the crawl space under the house. The concrete was no more than an inch thick and was only slightly wider than the blocks that rested on it. The work never would have passed inspection.

I intended to dig the most perfect trench ever dug. Stones and thick roots along the route made for slow going. Those obstacles didn't stop me in my mission, though. I measured the trench frequently, making sure it was precisely sixteen inches wide and just over four inches deep at its most shallow point. I even checked the trench with a level. I used a tamper to pack down the dirt and make the bottom of the trench as smooth as a pool table. Keeping the trench level on uphill ground and figuring out exactly where the "step-up" should go were tricky, but I got it done. The job took a day and a half, but when I finished, it was exactly the way I wanted it to be. The question, of course, was whether it would be good enough for Ben.

His opportunity to render judgment came when I returned to the farm a few days later. I was moving wheelbarrows of dirt away from the trench when Ben showed up.

"You really went to work after I left the other day," he said. "I came by Monday and saw you had finished the trench."

"I decided to go ahead and do it," I said. "I figured it wouldn't be that much more work for you if you had to correct something I did wrong."

"You didn't do anything wrong. It's perfect. Looks nice and level. You got the step-up right. I realized after I left Saturday that I told you the wrong thing when I said it should be fourteen inches wide. I was thinking about six-inch blocks instead of cinderblocks. I should have said sixteen inches. I see you even got that right. Are you sure you haven't done a foundation before?"

"Just did what you told me and some things I read in a book," I said.

"There's not another thing I need to do to it," Ben said. "You got that knocked out. All we need to do is get a cement truck in here to pour the footing, then get a block man over here to lay the cinderblock. After the inspector gives the OK I can start framing. We'll be in business."

Ditch-digging is supposed to be something any brute can do. But Ben's approval made me swell with pride. It was the first time he had given me a compliment that I considered unconditional, that wasn't offered to leaven criticism or just to give me encouragement. It was the first time I received his praise with full confidence that I had earned it.

+=— —=+

Ben amazed me over the next two weeks. I made a half dozen trips down to the farm during that time. I saw him only once, when I helped nail a plywood sub-floor to the sill and joists he had built on top of the foundation. But it was evident he had been there much more than that. Either he had been there or elves had, because the dining room rose as if by magic. One day I found the wall studs with their top plate and footing done. Another day I found the rafters and ceiling joists in place. Then the rough openings for the windows and doors had been framed, complete with headers. The decking for the roof appeared. Finally, the plywood sheathing showed up nailed to the frame. My major contribution was to cheer Ben on via the messages I left on his telephone answer machine. I called each time I visited the farm and found the latest piece of miraculous progress. "Hi, Ben. It's me," I would say. "I was down there today and saw you've framed the walls for the dining room. It looks great." Or I'd say, "I saw you got the rafters up. I really appreciate all the help."

A large room was added to the house, and, other than laying the foundation, Ben did it single-handedly. I couldn't imagine how he managed it.

My next job was installing the doors and windows. My plan called for using sliding-glass doors for both entrances to the room from the decks. But Ben convinced me to use French doors on the side toward the front. "That's the side everybody will see," he said. "French doors will look so much better."

I installed the room's four insulated, double-hung windows. They were arranged in east-west parallel pairs. A window on the east side of the room was directly across from a window on the west side. The eastern windows invited the morning to settle comfortably into the breakfast nook. The western windows afforded a view up the hill to the horizon where the sun would redden and disappear in the evening. The only remnant of my vision of wall-to-wall plate glass was a five-foot-by-five-foot picture window at the far end of the room. That window faced the south, ensuring sunshine would stream in all day. Add the French doors to the east and the sliding-glass door to the west and the result was a room full of light. That's what I had in mind when I first drew that glass-walled spaceship of a dining room.

Ben came over one day after I had all the windows and the doors in. We walked through the room and around the outside. We didn't say very much. We just admired it. We had settled on building two decks. One would span the back of the house, with sliding glass doors opening onto it from the dining room and the master bedroom downstairs. The other deck would extend from the dining room and wrap around the house to connect with the front porch. People wouldn't have to drive or walk around back to have easy access to the room. Part of the front deck would be in the shade of the big pine tree. I imagined what it would be like sitting on the deck while a gentle breeze whispered through the pine and cooled the deck.

Ben interrupted my reverie when our brief tour ended.

"Now this is a room you'll get some use out of," he said. "Aren't you glad you did this instead of that little-biddy thing you were going to do at first?"

"Yes, Ben," I said. "This is ten times better than what I had in mind."

"You know, I have to laugh when I think about how bad that room you wanted was. You were insisting so much on doing it that I wondered if I should let you just go ahead and do it. But then I thought, Naw, I can't let John do something he'll regret as soon as he's done it. So I just tried to steer you in the right direction no matter how headstrong you got about it. Man, you wouldn't have had room to breathe the way you had it drawn up."

Ben teased me mercilessly about that room. Every chance he got, he reminded me of how absurd and useless the room I wanted to build would have been. But I didn't mind the ribbing. I could even look back and laugh at myself. That's a lot easier to do when you know you've done the right thing in the end, whether through coercion or because you finally came to your senses.

CHAPTER 11

For a few years back in the mid- to late-1970s, the sight of a grandchild with a tape recorder made African-American elders think about getting their affairs in order. Those were the years when *Roots* was a national phenomenon. The book's author, Alex Haley, lectured across the country and appeared on television urging blacks to do what he had done in tracing his family's history all the way back to its African roots. Talk to your grandparents and your great-aunts and uncles, Haley said. Get them to tell family stories as far back as they can remember. Ask them what stories their grandparents told them. Get their voices and their stories on tape, he said. And do it right away, because they won't be around much longer, and when they are gone, valuable links in history's chain will be broken. So millions of young blacks got cassette tape recorders and went to visit the oldest relative they knew. And millions of old folks, who were not unaware of this latest cultural fad, knew at once that someone believed they didn't have much longer to live.

I was one of those tape recorder-toting searchers intent on rooting out my family's past. The memory came back to me while I worked on the archway that replaced a wall and opened the farmhouse living room into what had been the dining room.

I was reminded of my recording session with my grandmother because it had taken place in the living room. I didn't know how many years ago I had done the interview. I didn't know where the tape was. I knew I had it somewhere. Surely I hadn't thrown it out. How could I have? It was the only recording of my grandmother's voice that I knew of. It was important. I must have stored it away somewhere. But, as with most things I owned, the fact that it was important enough for me to store away didn't mean I would ever find it.

⊹═ ═⊹

I got lucky. I found a box of old cassette tapes at the bottom of a stereo cabinet in the space where record albums were supposed to be kept. Almost all of the cassettes were of music I had taped, either from the radio or from records. But after rummaging around in the box I found what I was looking for. There, loose and with no cassette case to protect it, was the tape of my grandmother. On one side of the cassette I had written, "Julia Fitch (Grandma) 82 years old." The other side read, "Recorded 3-1-78." That was more than twenty years ago. I couldn't remember the last time I listened to the tape. Like the vast majority of Alex Haley wannabees, I didn't ever get too far down the family tree's trunk, much less to the roots. It was something I always intended to get back to, to take time off to get it done, but never did.

The tape was only thirty minutes long. That surprised me. I didn't remember much about the session with Grandma, but I had thought it was more than half an hour. She must have had more than thirty minutes worth of stories for me. I must have had more than thirty minutes worth of questions. But I knew I had made only one recording with my grandmother. This half-hour tape was it.

March 1, 1978, must have been a cold day. Otherwise, the interview would have taken place out on the front porch, with Grandma sitting in a rocking chair, which was much more conducive to the storytelling and reminiscing I was after. But I was sure we had sat in the living room. My battery-powered cassette recorder had a microphone with a little stand. It was pointed at my grandmother. I remember my Aunt Helen, who was living with Grandma back then, was there with us.

I put the cassette in the tape deck of my stereo system. When I pushed the "PLAY" button the voice that came out was like the chattering of a chipmunk cartoon character played at high speed. There was no way to understand a single word. I thought the tape must have deteriorated over the years until it was useless. I had let this link to my grandmother rust into dust.

But then I remembered my cassette tape recorder. It had a variable-speed playback. I put the tape of Grandma in and set the playback at the slowest speed. When I pushed the "PLAY" button this time, I heard my grandmother's voice strong and clear, speaking to me from twenty years ago. Hearing her voice, I saw her as she was in her early eighties. She was a woman who never grew fat, but rather shrank back into herself as she aged. She wore glasses with large lenses and wide frames that made her face look narrow. Her steel gray hair was always curled or in curlers. A colorful house dress was her daily uniform. Grandma talked and chewed gum at the same time. I remember that gum-chewing had replaced her snuff-dipping by then, but I'm not sure whether she gave up snuff for health reasons or to dispense with having a spit cup around.

I had started the interview by asking where she was born.

"Well, I was born . . . I guess we'll have to say it was Jackson, because it was right at Jackson," she said. "Oh, wait at minute. We'll start on your great-great-grandpapa.

"Your great-great-grandpa was a slave. He would never see none of his grandchildren. He was blind. But he was a nice old man. But as time rolled on, as we growed up, he would tell us stories about what happened, you know, in slavery times. I can remember some of the stories. Do you remember the general, what they call General Sherman?"

"Yes, ma'am," I heard my younger self say.

"He was coming to the South. Well, my grandfather was staying with old mistress and old marster. That's what they called
them. He was just a twelve-year-old boy. And when they heard
that Sherman was coming through, he had to carry the horses
down into the pines to hide 'em, to keep the soldiers from killing
them. He carried those horses down there—he said he went way
down in them pines. And when he come back, the soldiers had
poured out all the syrup and knocked old mistress in the head.
They didn't kill her.

"And he said the colored people were running so, and the soldiers were trying to show the colored people that they were free.
But they was scared. They didn't have sense enough to know it."
At this point, early in the tape, I saw Grandma would give me no
neat narrative. How could she as she retrieved moments stored
away in her memory over a span of more than seventy years? She
went about it as if putting together a large, complex puzzle. The
pieces that most obviously fit together came first—perhaps corners and edges. There were clusters—the blue of the sky, the
leaves of a tree. And sometimes she put down a piece that seemed
to come out of nowhere, but that made sense as she found the
other pieces to put around it. Grandma let me know she was
moving to other pieces by saying "time rolled on." But time did
not roll in a straight line. It moved like a pinball, bouncing from
place to place.

"So time rolled on," Grandma said. "These old people—his
ma and father, real Christian people; there were some more
Christian people who were slaves, too—the marster and mistress,
or whatever they called them, would give the slaves a house that
would have one room to enjoy theyselves. But marster and mistress didn't know their slaves were praying. My grandfather said
those old people got pots, pans and beat 'em to keep up noise.

"He said he told his playmates, 'They goes in that house once
a week. I'm going to see what they doing.' And he went and
peeped through a place where he could see them people shouting and praying. He said some of 'em was crying, they was
shouting and praying. They was praying for the Lord to help

their people, you see, because they were bowed down in slavery.

"From then on, he said, things was starting to get just a little bit better. He was a very religious old man, and he believed. . . . He said he knowed the Lord heard those old people's prayers, and things began to get just a little bit better, gradually. Didn't get better all at once. Times was tight for a long time.

"But as time rolled on . . . I can't think of all my grandpapa said, 'cause he told me a lot of things that would do you some good if I could think about 'em, but I can't think about 'em.

"But he was a very religious old man . . . and very good. He knew about slavery. But, now, the tight times, I don't know much about that. But my grandpapa lived for a long time. I think grandpapa was about. . . . He was well up in age when he died. But I do know this, that he believed that the prayers of them old people brought about some of the things that happened since then. He believed that before he died. And I believe it too. I really do.

"But we have to jump from there, 'cause I don't know much about slavery. I read a lot about it. I read a lot about the African people. I used to teach Sunday school—that's been years ago—I taught Sunday school about four years. And my Sunday school book, there on the back of it, said, 'Ethiopia shall soon stretch out her hands to God.' I've never forgotten that. And I consider the black people as the Ethiopians."

I heard myself cut to the chase in my search for African roots. "Did you know any people or did your grandfather know anybody who actually had been born in Africa or could remember it?" I asked.

"I can't remember if my grandpapa told me anything about anybody was born in Africa," she said. I felt a twinge of disappointment listening to the tape. I must have felt it twenty years ago, too. "I can't remember, because that's been a long time. I can't remember that—if he told me about anybody was born in Africa. But his mother and father, I know they were slaves, and he growed up in slavery. But before he got grown, the colored folks was freed—before he got grown. And he was a young man in slavery time. But I don't know of anyone.

"I read about 'em now; I read a lot about it. If you read *Roots*, you read all about that. And it's so many people now is searching for that, asking where they come from, want to know their ancestors. And some of them are going to Africa to find out. Probably, if you'll be able to go to Africa, probably you'll find out a heap about the African people.

"But you see, all of us didn't come from Africa. None of us that's here now come from Africa. I heard a man talking to a reporter, and the reporter asked him if he wanted to go back to Africa. He said he didn't come from Africa. And we didn't. We were born here in America, you see. We didn't come from Africa. But we would like to know more about it if we could. We'd like to find out more about it.

"I get forgetful, but I read a lot about the African people. I read books as long as my eyes were fair to see good. Any book that I find had something about Africa in it, I'd read it, because I wanted to know about it. But as a race, we are not Africans. You see Africans' pictures . . . you look at our pictures. We don't favor one another. Because we didn't come from there. African people could be our ancestors. We don't know. We can't claim 'em because we didn't come from there. Because the African people are not like us. They don't talk like us. I heard them talk sometime. And that's why I say we shouldn't consider ourselves Africans. We are *Americans*."

Her voice was full of vehemence as she spoke that last sentence. I wonder now if her words were aimed at me and my efforts to tie myself to Africa. She reminded me of a man from Cameroon I once met. He said many of the black Americans he met were in love with all things African and wanted so much to go back to live in the motherland. "But you cannot do it," he told me. "You are not Africans anymore."

I asked Grandma what she remembered about her childhood.

"Well, I was born. . . . I'd rather say Jackson because we were not far from Jackson," she said. "My childhood, it was very good. I can't say that I had no whole lot of hardships in my childhood. My daddy was a working man. And he was a sensible man. He knew how to prosper. In all of it, I had a happy childhood. I can't say no tragedy that happened to me that's worth recalling, from my childhood on up.

"I had four sisters. No, wait a minute. I had three sisters and two brothers. And we grew up together on the same farm. All of us married off the farm. I have not so much to relate about my childhood. It was very nice."

I asked her about going to school when she was young.

"Well, that was nice, because I was easy to learn. I went to school a while. I went to school long enough to help the teacher teach, you see. I always did like to do whatever I was doing well. And I liked to learn my lessons well. And by that I was always picked at the schoolhouse as one that would do the jobs good. That's the truth. I'm not saying that in no boastful way.

"They didn't have schools then like they do now. When you got to the ninth grade, you had done finished your high school, you see. And after I got to that grade, I could have went to Tuskegee. That's where my people wanted me to go. They wanted me to go to Tuskegee—to go to the college, you know."

This surprised me. I didn't remember anything about Grandma having the opportunity to go to the Alabama college founded by Booker T. Washington.

"But I just didn't want to go," Grandma went on. "I didn't have teaching in my mind because I didn't want to be bothered with no bunch of children. I didn't want to teach.

"But my father bought a trunk—a new trunk. My mother made up my clothes and they packed them, and I kept a'telling them I didn't want to go. You see, what good would it have done me to went on to Tuskegee where he spent his hard-earned money on me to give me an education, and as soon as I come out go and marry and have a house full of children? What good would it have done me? But I could have done it. My parents were generous enough to let me go on to college if I wanted to, and they were able to do it. But I just didn't want to go. And that's about as far as it goes, 'cause the rest of my childhood was very nice. I had a happy childhood. I had a wonderful mother, and a wonderful father."

"What was your maiden name, before you married Grandpa?"
I asked.

"McKibben. My daddy, his name was Rance McKibben. I had
one brother, his name was Edward. I had another brother named
Walter. I had three sisters: Essie Mae, Clara, and Susie. That consisted our family. A whole lot I could tell you if I could remember. But these eighty-two years have knocked it nearly out. Can't
remember things like I used to."

"When you were young, was there much interaction between
white people and black people? Did you play with white kids at all?"

"Oh, no. I never did play with no white kids. I don't say that
I couldna did so, but I never did. I didn't think that they . . . it
wasn't like it is now, you see. But they would come around and
sometimes want to play. But in them times, the colored people
didn't think the white people wanted their children to mix up
with the black people. I'm not saying the white children didn't
want to, because they would come around us. But I never did
play with them much. It wasn't no distinction between us that
made us not want to play with them, you see. But we just had
been taught that they didn't want their children to play with us.
So we didn't bother with them."

The cassette player clicked, signaling the end of the first half of
the tape. I turned it over and started it again, listening to the
sound of fumbling until I heard my voice again.

"How did you and Grandpa meet?"

"Let's see. I ought to know that." Grandma's laughter spilled
from the tape. That made me think of Grandma's sense of humor.
She had come to see the world as a comical place. The young
woman who had refused to smile at the camera for that picture in
the front yard had grown generous with her smiles. "Where did we
meet at?" she asked herself. "Oh, I know where we met. He had a
sister. . . . That's funny. I don't know whether I ought to tell that
or not. But he had a sister named Roxie. Me and her was going to
school together. And she told me her brother wanted to see me.
And I had never seen him, you see. I had never heard tell of him.

"And time rolled on, and it rained one day, and he come after his sister. And his sister Roxie told me, she said Buddy had come after her. And she said, 'Come here to the window.' And I thought I was so much more grown than him, you see. I went to the window and looked and said, 'Is that the little old boy you was talking about?' I said, 'He ain't nothing but a child.' I turned around and went on back and sit down." Grandma laughed again, and she was joined in the laughter by Aunt Helen.

This was slightly different from the story of her first sight of Grandpa I remember her telling me when I was a child. I have to trust her memory. It's her life, after all.

"I didn't see no more of him for a long time," Grandma continued. "The next time I seen him, he was at the church, at Macedonia. I didn't pay him no attention then. I thought I had my pick of boys, you see, 'cause I was kind of independent too. And we would have fights sometimes. And what I thought was so funny, we would have fights, and we wrote to each other then. He'd come to the house, and we'd have a fight sometime that evening." Grandma laughed. "He'd go home. And in two days I'd get a letter from him and he'd get one from me."

While I listened to more of Grandma's laughter, I tried to imagine Grandpa sitting down to write her a letter. It was hard to picture. Were they love letters, or just a logical laying out of the arguments to show that he was right? I should have asked Grandma about that, but I hadn't.

"Time rolled on like that," she said, "and we went on like that for a long time. I think we were like that for five or six years. We went together five or six years before we took a notion to marry. But one thing, I was always like this about anybody: If you don't know a person, you don't need to marry them. I like to know their faults, and their likes and dislikes. If you know that before-hand, you save yourself a whole lot of trouble. So, our life together was very nice."

"How old were you when you got married?"

"I was twenty years old. And he was just a couple of months older than me. I was twenty years old in October and he was twenty years old in August."

"Was that unusual? Didn't girls usually marry men who were much older than they were?" I obviously had in mind the stereotypical picture of girls back then marrying young, with the prime catch being an old widower who owned land and offered security.

"In those times, girls was always trying to marry somebody whose age was pretty close to theirs," Grandma said. "If they married somebody whose age was seven, eight, or eighteen years older, they say she married an old man. But it's not so now. All that old man got to have is some money, and she gon' marry him. I would do it myself if I was young." There was lots of laughter over that. "So that's that. They didn't want to marry no old man then, but now it don't make no difference. They see if he got some money. And I don't blame 'em."

"What year was it when you got married?"

"I'd have to look in the Bible. I don't know."

"Do you want me to go get the Bible?" Aunt Helen asked. Then there was the sound of her walking up the stairs.

"Did you live in Jackson when you first got married?"

"I never lived in another town in Georgia. But after we had been married a while, your grandfather went to Pennsylvania. He stayed up there a while and worked. And he didn't like it up there."

Here was another surprise, thanks to my faulty memory. I had forgotten she told me anything about Grandpa going up North to find work. I wondered where he went to work. In a Pittsburgh steel mill? In a Philadelphia naval yard? How would things have been different if he had stayed and sent for his family? What would my life have been like growing up in the industrial North instead of the small-town South?

The tape rolled on, and so did time.

"He come back to Georgia and went to Florida," Grandma said. "He went down there a while, and he sent for us, and we stayed in Florida seven years."

"What did he do in Florida? What kind of work did he do?"

"Well, he done construction work."

The story was interrupted. Aunt Helen had returned with the Bible. I heard the sound of pages being turned. Grandma was leafing through the family's history, the record of marriages, births, and deaths. Who had that Bible now, I wondered.

"You asked what year I was married?" Grandma said.

"Yes, ma'am."

"Nineteen and fourteen." I did the math. If Grandma was twenty in 1914, she would have been born in 1894. But if that was correct, she would have been eighty-four in 1978, not eighty-two. Which was correct? Who knows?

"Did Grandpa ever serve in the army?" (Why did I ask that question at that point? Maybe it was the marriage date's proximity to World War I.)

"No," Grandma said. "He had a mark on his head, where he was hurt once, and he didn't never have to go."

Aunt Helen disagreed. "He told us that he had an honorable discharge," she said. "He went, but he had an honorable discharge."

"Well, that wasn't so," Grandma insisted. "In that time, boys and men didn't want anybody to know that they were turnt down. See what I mean? They thought it was something to go into the army. And that's why he would say that. He didn't want anybody to know he was turnt down, you see." I had to side with Aunt Helen on that issue. In the storage shed's loft I once found a photo album with pictures of Grandpa in uniform.

"What was living in Florida like?"

"It was nice. Oh, that was a beautiful place. Delightful climate and wonderful people. I loved it."

"What part of Florida were you in?"

"Jacksonville. I had three children was born down there. Your Aunt Helen was born down there. Bessie and Marie. It was a beautiful place. I loved it. But after the Depression come on, you couldn't get nothing to do. But your grandpa, he didn't want to leave. He wanted to stay down there."

Again, this description of the family's sojourn in the Sunshine State didn't quite square with my memory of stories she had told me when I was a child. And she didn't even mention the falling fish or the house fire. I later asked my mother and two of her sisters if they remembered the incidents. They did.

The story continued on tape. "What was the Depression like?"

"That was bad," she said. "You couldn't get nothing to do. Some places you had to stand in line to get things. It was like that here. It was like that every which-a-where. Depression is a very bad thing. I hope it don't come back, not while I'm here, because you can have money and it won't do you no good. I've seen times when you had to stand in line to get a little bucket of lard, or to get a little sugar."

"So you came back here during the Depression?"

"Yes."

"Was that when you came to this place, to live on the farm?"

"No. When we came back, your great-grandfather, he was staying up there." The reference to "up there" meant just up the road from the farm. "And we came back here just about the time he was to gather his crop. We hoped him gather his crop, and then we moved up to Henry County, up to where your Aunt Clara stays." Listening to the tape, I smiled at Grandma's use of "hoped" for "helped." It was an old Southernism I hadn't heard in years.

"We stayed up there a year, and then we moved back down here to Jackson, out the other side of town. And then we moved from out the other side of town here, and we been here ever since."

"Was this house already here when you moved here?"

"Oh, no. They built this house for us. Ain't nobody ever stayed in it but us."

"Did Grandpa work on the house when it was being built?"

"Oh, no. They contracted to build it. We was the first people in here that got electric lights. Time rolled on, and we was the first people in here that got a radio. We were the first people that got a television. And we were the first people that got a telephone. Right here in this house."

"You mean the first people in Butts County?"

"No. Right here in this community right round in here."

"Did people used to come down just to listen to the radio and things like that?"

"Yeah, they come and listen to 'em. Now, I didn't tell you this before, but your great-grandfather was the first colored man in Butts County that owned a new car."

"What kind of car was it? Do you remember?"

"I have done forgot. It's been so long. But I knew it was pretty. And he was the first colored man owned a new car. Out in the country, you know. I'm not talking about doctors, people who stayed in town."

"He owned a lot of land, didn't he?"

"Yes, he owned about three hundred acres once, till he sold some of it. That's why I can't say it has been hard for me all of my life, because he worked hard, and we worked hard, but he was a good provider. He raised everything we ate."

"Did Grandpa like farming?"

"Oh, yeah. Yeah, he liked it. But after the boll weevils invaded this place, you couldn't make nothing." She was talking about the insect that ravaged cotton crops. "He loved the farm. I always did love the farm."

"I didn't love it," Aunt Helen piped in.

"What do you remember most about your children?"

"Oh, I remember they was pretty nice children, in a way. Had to beat 'em up every once in a while, but they were right nice children. I can say this: They were obedient children. I never had no trouble with none of them. Your Uncle James, I think he'll be sixty, and right now, he never give me a bad word."

"How many children did you have in all?"

"Ten. I had ten children. And I must say, they all are right nice children. Yes they are. I can't say nothing against them. They never was a whole lot of trouble for me. I never had to go get one of my boys out of jail. I never heard tell of them jumping on nobody fighting. And I think that's a pretty good record. They didn't give me one minute's trouble. Neither did the girls. I have to tell the truth on them. And they all are nice to me yet. All of 'em."

"You once told me a story about Uncle James and somebody else were in the army overseas, and you heard something on the radio about a big battle."

"Yes. I remember that. James was on Rose Island, out in the

Pacific Ocean. And I was sitting out there listening to my little radio. And the radio said Rose Island had been bombed. It like to have scared me to death. I sat there and prayed. I said, 'Lord, hope my child wherever he is on that island.' The next day I got a cablegram. It just said, 'Safe and well, James.' That was one of the happiest times for me.

"I've never had no cause to complain about my children."

The tape clicked with finality, cutting Grandma off right there. I felt I should have asked many more questions, conducted many interviews. If I had, I'd already know the things I was trying to find out about the land, the house, and the family. But I doubt Grandma minded being spared more of my questions. She probably thought she had pretty much covered everything that really mattered.

CHAPTER 12

Guilt pricked at my conscience each time I drove down to or back up from the farm. I passed right by the home of my closest neighbors, and I hadn't stopped once to introduce myself and meet them. They lived in a brick house on some of the property L. H. Cawthon bought from my grandfather. But I didn't know the couple who owned it now. My mother said they were Charles and Rita Kinney. I hadn't made an effort to get to know my neighbors at all. That bothered me.

I wouldn't have worried about it in the city, of course. During the times I lived in Atlanta, in Detroit, or in Washington, it was the rule rather than the exception that I didn't know my neighbors. It didn't matter if all that separated us was a fence dividing two land lots or a wall between apartments. The distance between the farmhouse and folks "next door" was the equivalent of about two city blocks. People who live that far apart in the big city are about as likely to get to know each other as people who live in different countries.

It's not supposed to be that way in Butts County. At least, it wasn't that way when I was growing up there. You knew your next-door neighbors, even if "next door" was a mile away. Your families probably belonged to the same church. The children rode the same school bus—unless, of course, one family was black and the other white in the era of segregation. Regardless of race, the children were playmates from time to time. If they got to be good friends, they wore a path through the woods or through the pasture walking back and forth to play with each other. Husbands stopped by at the end of their workday to talk about the weather or what insects were into the crops or how good their hunting dogs were. The wives visited bearing food and recipes. If one family had a television set and the other didn't, the women talked about "the stories" so the one without TV could vicariously follow the popular soap operas—"As the World Turns," "Days of Our Lives," "Search for Tomorrow."

Maybe things weren't that way anymore, even out in the country in Butts County. But I knew I should behave as if things still were that way, because the people who lived next door had been that kind of neighbors to my grandmother in the last years she lived on the farm. They stopped by from time to time to chat with Grandma for a while or just to check on how she was doing or to see if she needed help with anything. They owned a tractor, and the man would till the small field where Grandma planted vegetables. When she stopped gardening, he used the tractor to mow the grass and weeds so the farm wouldn't be completely overgrown. Mom said he never charged my grandmother anything for his work, though I'm sure she offered something from the garden harvest or a dish she cooked. Nothing was asked for; something was always given. They were neighbors, after all.

Sometimes I saw them outside as I passed by. They obviously enjoyed the outdoors. There was a pond in the back of their house. They had an expansive lawn they cut with a riding mower. And there was a garden to tend. If they looked up and saw me driving by, they waved. I waved back.

But I never did the neighborly thing. I never walked over to knock on the front door of their brick home to introduce myself. I made excuses to myself for not doing it. I was always in a hurry to get started with the work when I got to the farm. By the time

I was ready to leave I was grimy and sweaty—about as presentable as a horse that's been rode hard and put up wet. But those excuses were no more than that: they were excuses. The truth was that the neighborliness I learned growing up in a small town was withering from lack of use, like an atrophying muscle.

So I spent a few minutes of each trip to the farm feeling guilty about not meeting my neighbors. That changed one day in March.

It was one of those Georgia days we call false spring. We got the year's first demonstration of how perfect the weather could be. It made us believe—or hope, at least—that the sun would be as bright and the air as soft and warm for the year round. Plants began cautiously poking their heads up, like helmeted soldiers peeking out of their foxholes. The more brash and foolhardy flora took a risk just to be the first in full bloom. The moments of glory they gambled for didn't last if winter sneaked back in with a killing freeze for just a night or two.

But winter wasn't a worry as I worked inside the house that Saturday afternoon. It was so warm I opened two windows to create a cooling cross breeze. That was why I heard the pickup truck when it pulled into the driveway. I opened the front door and stepped out onto the porch just as a man and woman walked up the steps.

"You're John, aren't you?" the woman said. "Your mother told us you would be coming down here working on the house. I'm Rita, and this is my husband Charles. We're your neighbors over there."

I shook their hands and started in on my excuses. "I've been meaning to stop by and introduce myself," I said, "but. . . ."

Charles cut me off. "That's OK," he said. "Looks like you've been pretty busy. I drive by and see how much you've done. You're really fixing it up. It's looking good."

"I know you've been working hard over here," Rita said. "I can hear you hammering away."

"I've gotten a few things done," I said, "but I still have a long way to go. There's a lot to do. You want to come inside and look around?"

They followed me inside. I showed them the things I had done, and told them what I was planning to do. They made encouraging comments at the appropriate places. We went back out onto the front porch when the tour was done.

"We spent a lot of time on this porch sitting and talking with your grandmother," Charles said.

"Mrs. Fitch was just a real nice lady to be around," Rita said.

"She enjoyed talking about anything," Charles said. "And who was the man who lived here, the one who was blind? I can't recall his name."

"That was Uncle Willie," I said. "He married my Aunt Helen." Uncle Willie was a deeply religious man who knew the Bible backwards and forward. He believed God gave him special powers to compensate for his blindness.

"That's right. Willie," Charles said. "That man knew his Scriptures. And he could talk about the Bible all day and all night."

"You remember the time y'all were talking about flying saucers and Mrs. Fitch made you quit?" Rita asked.

"I remember," Charles said. "But she didn't make us stop. We were talking about flying saucers and space aliens and whether they were for real. I said I believed they could be. There could be life on other planets. I asked Willie what he thought. And he said, 'I believe God can make all kinds of living things. He can make them here on Earth or any place else he wants to. So if I believe God can make them, I have to believe they can be real.' And I turned to Mrs. Fitch and I said, 'Well, what do you think about it?' She said, 'I'm going to get myself away from here. I don't even want to listen to y'all talking about it.' And she just got up and walked inside the house."

Charles and Rita both laughed, and I laughed with them. I could see Grandma doing that—not wanting to hear God pulled into something she considered nonsense.

My neighbors also told me how much they missed Grandma once she moved away from the farm. "It seemed like the house knew she was gone," Charles said. "It just started going downhill from there." The various renters who had been in the house hadn't been good neighbors, they said. Some were so noisy that even the distance between the houses wasn't enough of a buffer. None of them did anything to keep up the house or look after the land. Charles told me he cut the grass in the field once and found it littered with bottles and cans.

They asked if I planned to go back to renting the house after I finished work on it.

"No. I'm doing this strictly to get the house back into shape and to keep the property in the family," I said. "And I'm enjoying the work and finding out things about the house. I'd like to learn as much as I can about the history of the house and the land. I'm hoping to find out who built the house and track down more information about who my grandfather bought the land from and who bought land from him."

Rita gave me a quizzical look. "You know who that was, don't you?" she asked.

"I know one of the Cawthon brothers was involved," I said.

"It was Bear Cawthon," Rita said. "That was my daddy."

It pays to know your neighbors.

+►=◄+

The unexpected had a way of just jumping out at me around that time. It was coming on to spring, and nature began showing me the new order of things, showing me the place I had taken in the still-evolving history of the house and the land even as I sought to unravel that history. At times I was convinced I had stepped onto the stage as less than a bit player, a mere nonspeaking extra who wanders through scenes as the plot plows ahead. At other times, I saw myself becoming part of the story and changing it, diluting the details I wanted to gather in their purest form.

One day I looked out into the front yard and noticed two places where I had worked up a lot of sweat in the winter cold. I had spent a few hours ridding the yard of two large mimosa trees that were antagonists in my mission to re-create my grandmother's

flower garden. I didn't remember them being there in my childhood. They were squatters who sneaked in and put down roots
while no one was looking. They had to go: "Out damned spot!
Out, I say—One; two: why, then, 'tis time to do't."

I took hedge clippers to the trees' smaller branches. I moved on
to cutting larger limbs with a saw. I cut the trees down to stumps.
Then I dug around the stumps with a mattock. When I got down
to the large, deep roots, I chopped them with an ax. I thought I
had loosened the stumps enough to just lift them out of the hole.
I hadn't. They were still anchored, as if the ground around them
was concrete. Finally, I wrapped one end of a heavy chain around
a stump and secured the other end to my pickup truck. I engaged
the tree trunks in games of tug-of-war. The truck pulled the chain
taut. Its fat tires spun in place, throwing up plumes of red dust.
The stump did not budge. I backed up, relieving the tension in the
chain and allowing it to rest on the ground. I shifted into a forward gear and pushed the accelerator to the floor. The truck
lunged ahead, catching the stump off guard. The stumped moved
but did not give up its hold. I repeated the maneuver several times
until the stump finally popped from the ground. It had a large and
long root that went straight down from the tree, like the root of a
tooth. I found the same when I pulled up the other stump.

The trees were gone for good. They left wounds in the earth
that would fill up on their own and heal over time. Or so I
thought. But on a spring-like day I saw the mimosas green and
flourishing, rising from the holes out of which I thought I had
pulled life by the roots. Nature continues life's circular storyline;
we break the cycle through extraordinary effort or extraordinary
stupidity or both.

Those were also the days when I decided to undo some of the
damage I had done to the land while working on the house.
Large piles of debris—lumber, windows, pipes, bathroom fixtures—had accumulated. They were ugly and pressed down on
the earth, squeezing the life out of the soil. I rented a large trash
container that would be dropped off, filled with the debris, and
hauled to the dump.

The largest pile was on the house's north side, wedged between the driveway and a weedy field. I dismantled the mountain piece by piece, lifting a stud or sink or drywall and carrying it to the dumpster and tossing it in over the edge. As I worked my way to the bottom of the pile, I found that it wasn't as hostile to life as I had thought; it was, in fact, a harbor for life. Termites ate their winding tunnels into the lumber. Plump grub worms curled themselves into balls whenever I removed anything that served as their hiding place. When I got to the very bottom of the pile, I encountered the top of this ecosystem's food chain. Mice scurried out in every direction, from nests fashioned out of bits of paper and grass.

Dusk was settling by the time I had the pile cleared away. The spot where the debris had been was moist and bare, except for some small matted plants that looked like bean sprouts. As I stood on the front porch steps admiring my clean-up work, two owls swooped down out of the dim light and landed in the short grass near the big bare spot. When the predators gained the air again, I saw the body of a mouse dangling limply from the talons of each bird. A little later, this same pair (I presume) made another run to this market and again went home with carts full of food.

Well, I thought, I've restored the balance of nature. I've removed my clutter from the environment, and the owls are able to hunt again, as they were intended to.

But then I pondered that premise. I tried to look at it from the mice's point of view. They probably didn't see what I had done as restoring nature's balance. They probably saw it as an act of betrayal. First I created the perfect home for them, a place where they would be warm during the winter and where they could feast on grub worms when the weather turned warm. And it was a sanctuary where they were safe from their enemies. Then what did I do? I dismantled their home, stripped it down to the ground, leaving them no cover, leaving them at the mercy of those hungry owls. I could rhapsodize about cleaning up the environment all I wanted. As far as the mice were concerned, all I had done was turn them into supper.

This ecology stuff is a complicated business.

I wasn't done with the mice yet. Something had to be done about the grass growing up around the house. It was getting up to waist high. Most of it was what we called Johnson grass. I remember Grandpa putting us to work pulling it up in his corn field. It grew in long, tough blades with razor-sharp edges that cut our hands if we didn't reach down and grab it close to the ground before pulling it up, shaking the dirt from its roots, and tossing it out of the field.

I was better armed when I battled the Johnson grass this time around. I bought a garden tractor with a twenty-horsepower engine and a fifty-inch mower. But even with that much help, cutting the grass was slow going. It was a bumpy ride. I saw why when I got the grass cut down low. The furrows from the years of plowing the field were still there. They were evidence of the days Grandpa spent walking behind a mule, the plowshare slicing the soil open over and over until it looked like the grooves on a long-playing record. The furrows weren't loose soil anymore, of course. They were packed and protected by grass and weeds. The rows were plowed across the contours of the land to help fight erosion. I noticed that the ridges began gradually flattening when I kept the grass low. They were more exposed to the weather. The rain wore them down.

The second time I cut the grass was memorable. It was low enough that the garden tractor could move at a decent clip. The mower cut the new growth of grass and chopped up the dried grass that was still on the ground from the previous cutting. I was riding along near the far end of the field when I noticed mice running ahead of me as if they were being herded. They jumped frantically through the grass. When they leaped they looked like dolphins frolicking across the ocean surface. I don't know if I flushed them from one big nest or lots of little nests in the grass. All I know is that, once again, I set them running for their lives. Those mice must have thought I really had it in for them.

The warm weather brought out all kinds of pests, including litterbugs. After a winter closed up in their stuffy cars, people drove with their windows rolled down. And they threw trash out of those windows. Most of it seemed to find its way to the roadside in front of the farmhouse.

The trash infuriated me. Bottles, cans, cups, bags, wrappers, napkins—all the detritus of fast-food consumption piled up. I muttered to myself while picking it up, putting the garbage into a plastic bag while keeping a wary eye out for cars driving close to the shoulder. I thought about how inconsiderate people had become. People didn't do this stuff when I was growing up. They took more pride in themselves and their surroundings. I had never seen the roadsides of Butts County so littered in my life.

And then a memory returned, and I knew I was wrong. I *had* seen this same roadside covered with litter when I was a child. Grandma and I picked up as much of it as we could.

Large trucks loaded with cotton bales would pass the farm all day long. They carried the fall harvest to cotton mills. No matter how tightly the bales were packed, some of the cotton was blown from the speeding trucks. After a few days, the roadside was littered with cotton. It looked as if a heavy snow had fallen and started to melt. Grandma got two sacks—a large one for her and a small one for me.

We walked along the side of the road. Grandma kept me close to the ditch. She always stood between me and the road. The two of us gathered up this "trash" until the road was clean as far as my grandmother wanted to go. I don't remember what she did with this twice-picked cotton. Did she sell it for a few cents? Did she use it as stuffing for a pillow or a homemade doll? Or did she spin it into thread? I don't know. I just remember that she saw the trash someone left in front of her house and found a way to use it.

✦━ ━✦

Rita Kinney surprised me several times on that warm, spring-like day when we first met. The initial surprise was the closeness of the relationship she and her husband had developed with my grandmother. They were more than good neighbors. They looked after her. They spent time with her. They got to know her. I was jealous of them in a way. They knew her in the years near the end of her life when I was mostly away from her. I lived in Washington for some of that time. I was in Atlanta for most of it. Wherever I lived, I didn't see very much of Grandma. Rita and Charles had a closeness to her that I didn't have during those years, and it wasn't just a mater of being her neighbors.

Of course, she surprised me with the news that the man who sold the land to Grandpa was her father. I had known that a Cawthon had bought land from my grandfather, but now I understood her to say L. H. Cawthon was the one who *sold* the land to Grandpa. At first I thought she said L. H. Cawthon was her grandfather. She was about my age, so I assumed we were dealing with parallel relationships: it was my grandfather who bought the land, so it must have been her grandfather who sold the land. Learning that that assumption was faulty led me to another assumption: The transaction that took place almost sixty years ago was not between men of equal age. L. H. Cawthon, the younger man, sold land to my grandfather, the older man. That might seem irrelevant, but I considered it a significant detail as I tried to figure out what the relationship between the two men might have been.

"I'd like to talk to you sometime about your father and about how things went with the land between him and my grandfather," I said.

"I'll be happy to tell you what I can," she said. "But a lot of this happened before I was born."

Rita had a final surprise for me. She seemed surprised that I didn't know who she was. "You were in school with my sister, Pam, weren't you?" she asked.

"Yes," I said. "I remember Pam Cawthon. We had lots of classes together."

I did remember Pam. We were in the same graduating class at Jackson High School. I transferred there in the second year of desegregation of the local school system. I was one of about two dozen black students in a school with more than seven hundred white students that year. Many of the whites didn't hide their hostility toward us. But Pam was among those who were courteous or even friendly. She was attractive, personable, and a brilliant student. Pam and I were voted "Most Likely to Succeed" by our senior class. Well, they were half right. Pam became a bank vice president.

But whatever our shared experiences in the classroom, I never got to know Pam. I can't remember seeing her anywhere except at school-related activities. I didn't know which one of the town's several Cawthon families she belonged to. And even if I had known she was the daughter of L. H. Cawthon, it wouldn't have meant anything to me. I didn't see his name on a deed regarding Grandpa's land until almost thirty years later.

So I had never connected the dots. Now I tried to do that belatedly and get a picture of what it must have been like when Grandpa and "Bear" Cawthon talked about the sale of the land, or when they went through that odd transaction when my grandfather paid one dollar for property he already owned. I couldn't get it directly from either man. Rita told me her father had died the previous year—the year I bought the farm.

Maybe what I know about his two daughters tells me something about L. H. Cawthon. Everything Rita told me and everything I heard from others indicated she and Charles treated my grandmother with kindness and respect. In an atmosphere of intolerance, Pam Cawthon had shown tolerance toward me and other black students in the early years of school desegregation. There must have been something in their upbringing that led these two sisters to behave this way. Was it something they learned directly from their father?

But I'm reaching. The things we do, the ways we conduct our lives, aren't always derived directly from our ancestors. We are often conscious contradictions of those who preceded us. We are no more able to look at our present to discern the past we do not know than we can look at our present to predict a future we cannot see.

Certainly, no matter what their relationship was in 1939, James Fitch and L. H. Cawthon could not have foreseen the future interactions of their children and grandchildren. Surely, the idea that the black man's grandson and the white man's daughter would attend the same school, sit in the same classrooms, and be photographed together in the school yearbook would have been beyond either of their imagining.

When the three of us finished talking that day and Rita and Charles were ready to go, I walked with them to their truck. Rita stopped at some bushes we passed on the way. "What kind of plant is this?" she asked me.

"You're asking the wrong person about that," I said. "When it comes to plants I'm about as ignorant as you can get."

"What do you think they are, Charles?" she asked her husband.

"I don't know," he said. "But they sure look nice."

They certainly were handsome plants. They had small leaves that were a polished green. And there were tiny, tight white buds hanging down like teardrop pearls.

"I wouldn't mind having a cutting from one of those," Rita said.

"You're welcome to a cutting," I said. "In fact, you can dig one up if you like. I'm probably going to thin them out when I get around to doing something about the yards."

"Maybe I'll come back and take you up on that," Rita said. She and Charles got into the truck and left.

I hoped she would take me up on my offer. It would be my first act of neighborliness toward them.

CHAPTER 13

I developed an appreciation for Ben's critical eye, especially when he cast it on someone else's work. The day we did a walk-through to see if the house was ready for the county inspector, he found a lot to be critical about when he looked at the plumbing.

"I guess I didn't look at this too carefully when I first came out here," Ben said. "This is sloppy work, and some of it's just plain wrong. Whoever did this didn't know a thing about what they were doing. Some people go to somebody's house to unclog a sink and then start calling themselves plumbers."

Ben proceeded to point out a host of problems: drain pipes that weren't plumb; pipes so crowded together they wouldn't fit inside the wall, shutoff valves inside the walls; pipes and fixtures that weren't secured to anything. "The biggest problem is that he doesn't have a P-trap for that washer drain line," Ben said. "You got to have a P-trap. You know what that is, don't you?" Ben said. I was tempted to wisecrack that a P-trap is some plumbing device that traps pee. But I didn't. I gave Ben a blank look. A P-trap is a crook in the line that keeps water in the pipes, he explained. It's like those J-shaped pipes under a sink. The water in the pipes keeps sewer odors from coming back

into the house. It blocks the pressure of the sewer gases.
And therefore the name "P (for pressure) -trap."

Ben made me look at the plumbing in a different way—not as
someone intimidated by the prospect of judging something he
knew nothing about, but as someone looking to see if something
made common sense. Even at that level, the work failed. Pipes
took roundabout routes for no apparent reason. When the
plumber decided he *had* to go in a straight line despite being
blocked by obstacles, he simply bowled over them, causing structural problems in the process. There wasn't a pipe that was a
direct source of water for any one fixture. Lines that branched off
of lines branched off of other lines. I could see Ben was right. This
jumble of plastic pipes might be worth a fortune as a piece of
modernist sculpture. But as plumbing it was junk.

"The inspector won't let you by on this," Ben went on. "It's a
good thing he won't, too, 'cause you're going to have problems
when you start putting up your drywall. And once you get the
wall closed up, it's just a matter of time until you're going to have
leaks inside the wall. If that happens, it's going to really cost you
some money to get it fixed.

"You had a plumber do this work?" he asked.

"Yes," I said.

"Who was he? Did you say it was somebody from down here?"

"No. There were two. The contractor hired both of them.
The first one just quit in the middle of the job. So the contractor
brought in a second plumber to finish it. Of all the work I've had
done, the plumbing is what I'm most dissatisfied with."

"Well, those plumbers took you," Ben said. "They took you
big time. I bet you went ahead and paid them, didn't you?"

I didn't say anything.

Bobby the Plumber must have enjoyed himself telling people
about his dealings with me. "I enlightened him that parsimony
can be a very expensive proposition," he probably said. "He was
so intent on prioritizing vis-a-vis frugality, that he was negligent
in failing to observe the axiom of caveat emptor." Or maybe he
put it plainly when talking among friends: "I stole the man's

money and had him saying 'Thank you' when I did it."

Going behind the plumbers to correct their mistakes and to do the essential things they failed to do looked like an enormous job, perhaps one that was too large for me. Ben had already done so much. I couldn't ask him to do even more work that I had made necessary by trying to get things done on the cheap. I became discouraged for the first time in a while. That feeling I had early on—the feeling that I had taken on more than I could manage, and that the job would never get done—came back to me.

But I didn't have time to waste on whining and self-pity. Indian summer had extended well into October, but the cold weather would come sooner or later. I didn't want to go through another winter with the wind whistling through the wide gaps and holes in the siding. I wanted to get the new siding on, insulation in the walls, and dry wall up. None of that could happen until the county inspector signed off on all the work that had been done. As Ben said, there was no way the house could pass inspection until the plumbing was fixed.

I went about the work with the same sense of determination I had when I set out to save the house rather than tear it down as other people were recommending. But this time I was armed with the lessons Ben had taught me, not the least of which was that hurrying is no way to get a job done quickly. I decided to take my time and make sure I was doing things as I wanted them done at each step along the way.

First, I sat down and made a list of things I needed to do. Reroute the water for the washer connections. Install a P-trap for the washer drain line. Reroute the water lines for the shower stall. Install braces for fixture inside of walls. Take shutoff valves out of walls. Check carefully for leaks and other problems.

I went through a checklist of supplies I would need. The number of feet of pipe had to be estimated. There were various connectors that would allow the pipes to make the needed twists and turns—elbows, Ts, couplings. I would need the glue to hold it all together.

Then I drew diagrams of where the pipes would go. This was

like a child drawing pencil lines in one of those complicated mazes. But with this one, going through the walls was OK. What I had to worry about was having too many pipes in one place or pipes that should be inside the walls winding up outside.

Before I started cutting pipes to move, replace, or cap them, I turned the water off at the meter. I also opened the two outside spigots and all the valves inside the house. This would allow as much of the water as possible to drain out before I got to work.

All this offered further proof that working on the house was not the mindless exercise some people thought. There were problems to solve. My available solutions had to adhere to the rules laid out in the housing code. Then I had to think through them and choose the one that worked best.

All of this was something I did in my spare time. There were people who did it for their livelihoods. They worked at it every day. They did their jobs and did them well. They took pride in their work. They earned every penny they were paid. They were out there. I just didn't look hard enough to find them.

Ben made suggestions on how to do the work. I considered what he had to say. I followed some of his advice. Sometimes I came up with alternatives I thought were better. I worked on the plumbing on weekends and any time I could make during the week after leaving the office. I always left the farm smelling of glue, with my hands stained purple from the solvent I used to clean the plastic pipes. I put on coveralls for crawling under the house, but somehow the dusty dirt seeped through to my clothes. It could be tedious work.

Ben dropped by one evening. He looked over what I'd done so far. He didn't say anything. I felt a little uneasy, as usual, and thought I'd better explain why I hadn't done some of the work the way he suggested. "I decided to move the shower and fixtures to the other side of the stall," I said. "That way, I could come directly off the feeder lines and around this corner instead of having to run them under the house and back up through the floor."

"Oh, yeah," he said. "That was a good idea. That's much better. You're doing a good job on everything. This is the way it

should have been done. There's nothing sloppy about this. Now
you're getting to where the inspector is going to have to pass you."

I just stood there and enjoyed it as the praise poured over me.
Ben's words alone were enough to make the work worthwhile.

The job was finished on a Saturday night. I started checking
things after the last piece of pipe was glued into the last coupling.
I walked around the house touching the pipes and shaking them
gently, like someone kicking the tires of a new car. Everything
seemed to be in order. It was time for the big test. It was time to
turn the water back on. I shut the valves inside the house and the
spigots outside. When I stood over the water meter in the front
yard, I hesitated for a moment. What happened after I turned that
valve would determine whether I had done a good job, whether
I had earned Ben's praise, whether I was back on track to get the
house weathertight before the cold weather arrived.

I turned the valve and walked toward the house. By the time I
reached the front porch, I heard the telltale sound of water spraying from pipes. It seemed thunderously loud, as if Niagara Falls
had found its way into the house. Water must have been pouring
from every pipe. I cursed to myself and ran inside to see where
these huge leaks were.

I found the problem in the first place I looked. The downstairs
bathroom was being soaked. There was water everywhere, but
there were no leaks. I had forgotten to shut the valves on the lines
for the bathroom sink. Without thinking, I ran into the bathroom
to shut the water off. The flexible feeder lines were hissing and
writhing like angry snakes, and the hot water line could deliver a
painful bite if I got in front of it. I managed to close that valve
without getting burned. But while I did that, the cold water line
was spraying me. My clothes were soaked by the time I got the
water turned off.

I laughed out loud. I laughed because I had forgotten to shut
the valves. I laughed because I realized that dashing into the ser-
pents' den had been unnecessary. I should have gone back to the
meter to turn the water off there. No fuss, no muss. And I
laughed because I looked ridiculous standing there with water

running down my face, my clothes sopping wet and my shoes making squishing sounds when I moved. I laughed because I could afford to laugh. The house fell silent as soon as the valves were shut. There were no big leaks. The pipes were holding. I had done a good enough job.

+≻= ≈+

After months of digging into the origins of the house, months of mining for nuggets of information that would yield the identity of Mr. M, I felt the thrill of hitting pay dirt.

It came in a call from a woman named Brenda King. She was with the Butts County Historical Society. She got the message I left on the society's answering machine. It was one of those machines that leaves you wondering whether it's working. The beep that was the cue to deliver your lines was about fifteen seconds late. I left one of those "If this thing is working please call me, but don't worry about it if it isn't working" messages. After a week passed with no response, I just forgot about it.

But the telephone rang at home one night, and the woman on the other end identified herself as Brenda King, with the historical society. She apologized for taking so long to respond.

I told her where the farmhouse was located, and I explained my search for its origins and for the identity of the man who left his signature inside the wall.

"You mean that two-story house out on Covington Highway?" she asked.

"Yes. That's it."

"I know that house," she said. "My daddy was a carpenter and he worked on that house. I remember he took me with him there several times and I played in the yard while he worked."

I held my breath, realizing this could be it. In the next moment I might know who Mr. M was; I might be on the way to finding out what kind of man he was. "What was your father's name?" I asked, praying all the while that the answer was preordained to be

George Mashburn or Mathews or Washburn or Whatever.

"He was a Britt," she said.

I thought about the signature inside the wall. I pictured the illegible writing of the last name and tried to extract "Britt" from the jumble. I didn't think it was possible. "What was his first name?" I asked.

"His first name was Elmer," she said.

It wasn't him.

She asked when the house was built. When I told her it was completed in 1940, she said, "Oh. The time I'm remembering was in the '50s. I don't think Daddy built the house. He just did some work on it. And I never knew Daddy to write his name on the inside of walls, either."

"Well, do you know of any carpenter named Mashburn or Mathews or Washburn who would have been building houses back in 1940?"

"No," she said. "I'm afraid I don't. Now, there were some Mashburns in the Pepperton community east of town, but I don't know that much about them."

"I'm trying to track down any information I can find about the house," I said. "Even where the lumber for building it came from."

"The building material probably would have come from one of two businesses," she said. "Either Barnes Lumber or Gilmore Lumber. Those were the two main ones back then. But both of them are long gone."

Brenda King seemed to be a walking, one-woman historical society. Ask her questions about Butts County and she could rattle off answers without having to look anything up. But she didn't hold the key to the house's secrets, at least not the one I was looking for.

However, my flirtation with solving the puzzle did inspire me to dig a little deeper. I thought some county records might hold the information I was searching for. Perhaps the names of the carpenters would have been recorded when the building permit for the house was issued. I called the building inspections office and asked how far back their records on building permits went. I was told the county didn't even require building permits until a few years ago. No luck there.

Where else might I find information about the house? I already had the property deed, which only added to the mystery with its one-dollar land sale between Grandpa and L. H. Cawthon. What other aspects of property ownership resulted in a paper trail?

Paying taxes, of course.

I called the tax commissioner's office and asked how far back their records of property tax payments went. I expected the woman to tell me about tax books left over from before the Civil War. "We've got them all the way back to the 1980s," she said.

Surely she meant 1880s. "Back to the 1980s? You don't have anything earlier than that?"

"How far back you want to go?"

"At least to 1940," I said.

"Oh, we don't have anything from back then," she said. "We've got some books in a display case in the lobby that go back into the 1970s."

The 1970s as ancient history? It was inconceivable to me that there would be no tax records older than that. "Are you sure that's as far back as the records go?"

"There may be some locked up in the courthouse, but I don't know if you can get to those. I'll tell you what. You can talk to the tax commissioner. That's Mrs. Hilda James. She can tell you what's over there."

I went to the tax office that afternoon. People were lined up to pay car taxes. Clerks behind glass partitions took their payments and typed the record into computers.

Tax Commissioner Hilda James and I had never met, but as soon as I introduced myself, she greeted me as if we were old friends. In a way we were. She knew my mother and my brother Fred, the prison warden and former county commissioner. As far as she was concerned, that was as good as knowing me.

"Fred and I worked together a lot," she said. Then she started laughing. "Every time I think about Fred I remember the story he told when he made a speech. He said one of your mama's friends was visiting and Miss Myrtle was telling her how well her children were doing. She said this one was working for the state legislature and that one was a lawyer out in California and this one worked for the phone company and that one worked for the newspaper. Then she said, 'And Fred is out at the prison.' And the woman said, 'My goodness! What did he do?'" Mrs. James shook her head as she laughed again. "What can I do for you?" she said.

I told her about the house and my search for its history. "I thought the old tax records would show something, but the secretary said you didn't have anything back beyond the 1970s."

"We don't have any older ones here," she said, "but there are some over at the courthouse. I don't know if they go back that far, but we can go have a look."

The tax commissioner was a lively woman. She was out of her chair and around her desk before I could tell her she didn't have to bother about walking across the street with me. I could ask someone at courthouse about the books. But she quickly ushered me out the door and across the street. As we walked, she talked about the plight of the county's records. "When I got here there were papers and books stacked up everywhere," she said. "We had so many tax books that the maintenance man took a mind to have them all hauled away. He didn't know no better. I came in and they were loading up a truck. I saved what I could and we put them away in the courthouse."

I thought about all that history being consigned to the dustbin of progress. If my luck so far held, the only books missing would be the ones I was looking for.

Once inside the courthouse, we went to the voter registrar's office. Mrs. James introduced me to the two men who were sitting at a desk across from each other. She explained what I was looking for. "Go right ahead," one of the men said. "All we've got is right in there." He pointed to a vault door with a combination lock. Mrs. James went over, lifted a handle and pulled the door open. "There's only one person who knows the combination, and he's gone so much we just leave it unlocked," she said.

The door opened into a large room. Piles of papers rose from the floor. The stacks—knee-high or higher—took up much of the space. A few were obviously surveyors' drawings of land lots. Most were official documents of indeterminate purpose. Large shelves lined three walls from floor to ceiling.

"They're up there," Mrs. James said. She was looking at a row of leather-bound red books on the top two shelves to our left, twelve to fifteen feet up. Each volume was about two feet high and four or five inches thick. They had gold lettering on their spines. Some read "Cash Book" while others were labeled "Tax Collections." All were dated by year or a span of a few years.

"What are cash books?" I asked Mrs. James.

"It used to be that everybody came in and paid their county taxes in cash," she explained. "The tax collector gave them a receipt and wrote their names in the book."

"That's what I'm looking for," I said. The books were dated from the 1930s to the 1970s. They were arranged haphazardly. There were a few consecutive years grouped together. Most were out of order. And there were years that were missing.

Mrs. James squinted and held her hand to her forehead as if shading her eyes from the sun. "I can't read what the dates are," she said.

I scanned the dates, looking for years I might be interested in. "There's 1938," I said, "and there's 1940, 1942, 1952 through 1956. The years I want are there."

"Well, we're going to need a ladder to get up there," she said. We looked around the room, but saw no ladder. We walked out and asked the men if there was a ladder to reach the top shelves. One of the men said he thought there was a ladder in the building, but he didn't know where it was.

Hilda James led me down the hall to another office. She leaned into the door and asked the secretary if there was a ladder in the courthouse. "We've got one," the woman said. "But the maintenance man takes it with him everywhere he goes. He's out now and probably won't be back before five o'clock."

I told Mrs. James I had a ten-foot stepladder at the farm, and offered to go get it. She looked at her watch. It was about four-fifteen. "That won't give you much time," she said. "We close my office at six o'clock. I believe we've got a ladder somewhere over there. Let's go back across the street and see if we can find it."

We marched back to the tax office. There was a six-foot aluminum stepladder in a supply office. "You can use this," Mrs. James said. "You go get the books you want to see and bring them back here. You can work at that table in the lobby. If you're not finished when we close, we'll lock you in and you can keep working. You can let yourself out when you're done and just leave the books in here."

I took the ladder into the vault and unfolded it in front of the shelves with the tax books. It looked as if the ladder wasn't high enough to allow me to reach the top shelf, but when I climbed up to the ladder's next-to-last step I was able to reach the books at the top. I pulled down the books for 1940, 1942, and one book labeled 1952–56. After signing a note listing the books I was taking, I headed back to the tax office.

Each of the books was heavy. Perhaps they were heavy because of all the cash they contained, I thought. They recorded all those dollar bills and coins brought down to the courthouse and counted out into the hands of the tax collector. There were no payments sent in after a tax bill arrived in the mail. These were face-to-face transactions where you could look the government in the eye as you gave it your money.

I stacked the books on the desk in the tax office. I opened the 1940 cash book first. In neat, legible script, someone had written columns of dates, names, and the amounts paid for various taxes—poll tax, state tax, county tax, county bond tax, and countrywide school tax—and, finally, the total tax paid. The ink on the pages had faded some, but it still was easy to read. I imagined the aroma of the open bottle of ink on the tax collector's counter. I could see the pen dipped into the ink and then put to paper.

The entries started in January. I slowly ran my finger down the pages, stopping when I saw names that were familiar—Carmichael, Fuqua, Maddox, Carter, Head, Whitehead, Greer, and others. The days and months passed beneath my finger. January, February, March, April . . . Time flew, and I saw no entry for my grandfather's payment of taxes. But then there he was. James Fitch. He paid his taxes on December 20 and was among the last to pay up that year. I looked across the columns. He had paid no poll tax, which did not surprise me. By paying the poll tax, you purchased the right to vote. It cost most of Butts County's taxpayers one dollar. Poll taxes eventually were struck down by the U.S. Supreme Court as unconstitutional barriers aimed at denying blacks the right to vote.

I read the payments Grandpa made in 1940: $13 in state tax, $55 in county taxes, $208 in county bond tax, $13 in countywide school taxes for a total of $289. That seemed an extraordinarily large tax bill for that time. But a closer look showed the figures weren't in dollars only. They were in dollars and cents. Grandpa's county tax bill that year actually was a grand total of $2.89.

Two dollars and eighty-nine cents. I wondered how grudgingly my grandfather handed over that money. Did he pull two crumpled and dusty dollar bills from his overall pockets and press them flat against the counter before counting out the eighty-nine cents coin by coin? And did the tax collector take the money in good cheer, or was he as dour and glum as the people who made the payments?

The 1940 book also had the payments for 1941. My grandfather's name didn't appear for that year. But I found him again in the 1942 book. He paid up on November 7 of that year. His tax payments increased by more than 20 percent, all the way up to $3.51. But that was because he paid the poll tax that year. I didn't think blacks voted at all back then. Did Grandpa pay his poll tax and then show up at the polls? Was this an act of defiance? I found him again in the 1952 book. This time his taxes were $4.22, without payment of the poll tax. Why had he not paid it that year? Had he been intimidated into not voting? Or was it a matter of money? Did he think paying more than five dollars in taxes was just too much, no matter what basic right that extra one dollar bought?

It was almost 6:00 P.M. when I finished going through the books. I tried to figure out whether the numbers told me anything useful. Could anything meaningful about the land or

Grandpa be reduced to figures written down and tallied? I was lucky to have the tax books at all. They almost had been tossed out. I looked back at the tax office secretaries typing at their computer terminals. They were storing the day's harvest of numbers. Forty, fifty, or sixty years from now my grandchildren will have an easier time finding records of my tax payments for the farm. They won't have to step into a paper-filled vault and climb up a ladder. They won't have to move their fingers past hundreds of names to find my name. The push of a button will retrieve all my county property tax records. They will have the numbers. But will the numbers tell them anything meaningful about me or about the land or about how I felt about the land? I think not.

╉━ ━╉

I was in good spirits as I drove down to the farm on a Friday night. Things were finally falling into place. I planned to spend the whole weekend in the house tying up loose ends and tidying up before the inspector came on Monday. And Ben would come over at some point to make a final check of the plumbing work I had done. As I walked up the steps to the front porch, I saw a page from a small notebook folded and stuck in the door. I pulled it out, unfolded it, and read it.

"John," the note began, "the work you did looks great. You did a good job. But I'm afraid we have another major plumbing problem. John, I believe we can take care of it. The house will never pass inspection unless it is done. I'll come back tomorrow to talk to you about it." It was signed "Ben."

My heart sank. Would I ever stop paying for the mistake of hiring the wrong plumbers? Was I incurring the wrath of an angry god of the Church of Preservation? Was there no balm in Gilead?

Calm down, John. Ben said it's something we can take care of. If it were a really big deal he would say so. If I had learned anything about Ben, it was that he's a straight shooter. If my work had made things into a mess, he would have not hesitated to say,

"John, you have made a bad situation hopeless. We have to dig up the pipes all the way back to the meter and start over again."

But Ben hadn't said anything like that. His note sounded a little weary, but not worried. There was no doubt in my mind that he would show up the next day ready to lay out the problem and offer his plan for solving it. I had no trouble sleeping that night. I was confident Ben would save me once again.

I began work in the house the next day before the morning sun had a chance to chase away the chill of a cold night. I looked over the plumbing, trying to find the major problem Ben had spotted. Nothing jumped out at me. For sure, everything looked 100 percent better than the work Bobby the Plumber had left. All the fixes Ben suggested were in place. Of course, a major problem doesn't have to be large enough to be seen. If you didn't know the intricacies of the workings of a huge passenger jet, you could inspect it for years without finding the one small piece—the one tiny screw—that had to be in place to keep the plane from falling from the sky. I decided I might as well relax and wait for Ben.

He arrived about an hour and a half after I began work. "Where's the fire?" he said. "You're getting started early."

We walked back to the downstairs bathroom. Ben explained what he had found. "I'm sorry I missed it before," he said. "I didn't even think to look for something so obvious. I should have known to check everything those plumbers did. When I was looking at your work yesterday, I just happened to notice the drain pipe from your shower and tub upstairs. He didn't put a P-trap in. I went under the house and looked at the drain pipe for your shower stall down here. Same thing. The pipe just came straight down into the sewer line. You've got to have P-traps on your drain pipes. Otherwise you're going to have sewer gas coming back into your house. The odor is going to be bad, and it could make people sick, too."

"Are there any other drains we're going to have to do?" I asked.

"You've already taken care of the washer drain with that in-line P trap," Ben said. "The ones for the sink will be underneath." Ben paused. "What about the toilets?" he asked. "What are we going to do about P-traps for them?"

It was another one of those Ben questions. But I didn't see it as a snare he had set for me. I thought of it as an exercise in Socratic teaching. I pondered for a moment, picturing the toilet with the relief of the curvy water line from the bowl to the drain. I thought of the water that stayed in the toilet bowl. "We don't have to worry about those," I said. "The P-trap for the toilet is built in."

"That's right. You got it," Ben said. He smiled with satisfaction, and so did I.

But both our smiles melted with what Ben said next: "Putting in the P-traps ain't no biggie. The real problem is that the plumber didn't put vent pipes in. He put in the one big vent pipe for the toilets, but you got to have all the drains vented. If you don't have 'em vented, you're going to have water draining real slow, and you'll have a gurgling sound. It can even make pipes burst if you don't have them vented."

I didn't know what Ben was talking about. At first, the word "vent" made me think of bathroom exhaust fans. But Ben took the time to explain it to me as if I were a seven-year-old. The vent pipes allow air to come in behind the water that flows down the drain pipes. Without that air, the water won't flow freely. Gravity pulls the water down, but what air there is in the pipe above resists being stretched toward a vacuum. The water is held back until pockets of air gurgle through the pipes and let the water lurch on through. Vent pipes were among the essentials the inspector would look for, Ben said. If the plumbing wasn't properly vented, it wouldn't pass inspection.

It seemed there were thousands of things unseen or taken for granted that made a house work. And it seemed that Ben Hamilton had taught himself all of them.

I didn't know what vent pipes were, much less that plumbing wouldn't work properly without them. No wonder I couldn't find the "major problem" I'd been looking for. It was as if I had looked at that huge passenger jet with absolutely no understanding of aerodynamics. I wouldn't have known the absence of wings meant the plane couldn't fly.

Venting the plumbing required putting in a system of pipes to carry air to the drain lines. Ben and I looked over the plumbing and came up with a plan. We each suggested configurations and discussed which ones would work best. Then we estimated the amount of pipe and other supplies we needed. Ben had other things to do until later in the day, so I went to buy the supplies and started on the work of drilling holes and putting together pipe.

Ben stopped by in the afternoon and assessed what I had done so far. He pronounced it good. I continued working while Ben was off again to take care of other business. I had gotten most of the work done by the time Ben got back that evening. We worked together for a while on the things that went a lot easier with two people than they would have with one. We were close to being finished when Ben had to leave for the night.

"You're almost there, John," Ben said. "Keep going the way you're going and the inspector won't have anything he can gig you on."

"I'm going to keep working," I said. "I was planning to spend the night anyway. I should be able to get everything finished tonight."

"You sure you don't want to wait?" Ben asked. "I can come back tomorrow afternoon to help with whatever needs to be done."

"I'll go ahead and get it done. I'll have it ready for you to come by and see if everything is OK."

"I'm not worrying about checking it," Ben said. "You've got the hang of it. You're doing everything the right way."

So Ben left me on my own. I felt a sense of accomplishment as I worked late into the night. And I thought about the way Ben and I had discussed what needed to be done and the way we had worked together. For the first time, I thought, we really worked as a team. We were two men with a common goal. We were equals. I was more than twenty-five years into adulthood, yet I felt I had done some growing up that day.

CHAPTER 14

I found answers to most of my questions about the Fitch family farm—including answers to questions I had not known to ask—in a single day. I found them in stories told on an ideal October day as warm and bright as my childhood memories of the farm. During a wakeful night spent in the unheated farmhouse, a night as cold and hard as the lives of the people who belonged to the land, I pondered what I discovered.

My Uncle Marvin, the youngest of the siblings at fifty-nine, was hosting the annual family get-together. As many of my mother's brothers and sisters as could make it would be there. It was an ideal opportunity to ask more questions about Grandpa, Grandma, and life on the farm. I had posed lots of questions already. Answers about Grandpa almost always included the observation that "Papa really provided for his family." It would be said at the beginning of the answer, as if the speaker wanted to emphasize it as the most important fact, or at the end of the answer, as if that was the thought the speaker wanted to leave me with. Questions about life on the farm invariably drifted off into anecdotes that left everyone laughing.

There was little laughter in the answers that day. The "Papa really provided for his family" qualifier was seldom invoked. I don't know what changed. Perhaps I had asked too many questions and everyone just wanted to be done with it all. Or maybe my questions set them thinking, and remembering.

It started with a simple question I asked after picking up Mom in Jackson and my Aunt Helen in the nearby community of Flovilla for the hour-long drive to Uncle Marvin's house in Atlanta. We were barely on the road when, looking straight ahead, I put the question in the air. "Did Grandpa ever grow cotton on the farm?"

"Papa started out growing cotton," Aunt Helen said. "But he grew peppers, watermelons, corn, and sweet potatoes."

"He raised a lot of different things he could sell," Mom added. "But he was a big cotton farmer back then. He had all kinds of equipment. He had a cotton planting machine, but somebody came and got it one time and never brought it back."

"He raised plenty of watermelons, too," Aunt Helen said. "Myrtle, do you remember that old house that was on the farm? I remember one year he grew so many watermelons he stored them in that house and filled it all the way up. And he made sure we didn't bother any of them either."

There was a brief silence, just long enough for me to consider a man who harvested a houseful of watermelons and then denied them to his children.

Aunt Helen broke the silence. "And we had five cows, too," she said. "We had to milk those cows every day."

"That's one of the jobs I hated," my mother said. "Getting up and milking those cows. Papa got up at 5:00 A.M. and worked all day. I had to get up to fix biscuits for him."

"We spent a lot of time in those fields, all of us," Aunt Helen said. "You remember that, don't you, Myrtle?"

"Yeah, I remember. We started out chopping cotton in the spring—taking that hoe and going down the rows."

"Did you just dig out the weeds?" I asked.

"No, it wasn't just weeding," Mom said. "You had to thin out the cotton plants and just leave the best ones."

"That must have involved a lot of bending over to be careful not to cut down the wrong plants," I said.

"Yeah, you had to be careful. It was hard. But then the next thing was bunching. I hated that worse than anything else. That began around the Fourth of July. I remember it was around July Fourth because everyone else would be going off and doing things for the holiday and I would want to go. But we'd be out there in those fields bunching. We had to take a hoe and clear the bunch grass and anything else from around those cotton plants. We just went down the rows. And then we started picking cotton in the fall."

I thought of my one experience picking cotton in the fields. I was fourteen years old, I think. That Saturday, Mom sent James, Fred, and me to go with some friends of hers who were experienced pickers. At the time, the going rate for picking cotton was three cents a pound. The very good pickers among those women made about ten dollars from a long, hot day of pulling the puffy, white cotton bolls from the plants and stuffing them into burlap sacks. My brothers and I picked a little over a hundred pounds between us, and divided about three dollars for the day. I believe Mom sent us just so we would know what picking cotton was like. It was some of the hardest work I had ever done, but my mother's recollection revealed that I had done the easy part. "So, did Grandpa let you go to school during picking time?"

"Oh, no," Mom said. "Papa put work first, ahead of school and everything else. On the days we did go to school he came and picked us up early so we could go home and help in the fields. I would be embarrassed sometimes. I remember I was absent working in the fields so much that the other children would tease me. The teacher would be calling the roll. When she said 'Myrtle Fitch,' before I could say 'Present,' someone would shout 'Out picking cotton!' and everybody would laugh."

"I remember the night Marvin graduated from high school," Aunt Helen said. "Papa wouldn't drive him over to the school for it. He wasn't even going to let him go. Marvin was just crying, he wanted to be there for graduation so bad. Bessie saved him that night. She called somebody to come pick him up and take him."

My Aunt Bessie was the fourth-born among the family's five girls.

"Papa didn't care nothing about going to school activities," Mom said.

"Not even graduations?" I asked.

"Not even graduations," my mother said. "He just never went, him nor Mama either."

"Now, Mama was the one that had some education," Aunt Helen said. "She was reading all the time. And she was real good at writing, too."

I thought of Grandma sitting at a desk scribbling poetry, or stacking up a novel's manuscript pages written out in longhand. But then Aunt Helen clarified what she meant.

"Did you ever see Mama's writing?" she asked me. "She had the prettiest handwriting you'd ever want to see."

We were all silent for a while. Then Aunt Helen spoke again.

"You ever tell him about Buckeye Hill, Myrtle?" she asked. "You ever heard about that, Johnny?"

"No," I said. "What was that?"

"Buckeye Hill was a piece of the land Papa owned over toward Jenkinsburg," Mom said.

Jenkinsburg is a community just north of Jackson. It seemed to me that Grandpa would have had to have more than 103 acres for his land to stretch that far. "Was this a plot of land separate from the farm?" I asked. "Was it not included in the land Grandpa bought from Mr. Cawthon?"

"No, it was all the same land," my mother said. "It was about a mile from the house, I guess. I don't know why they called it Buckeye Hill. I just know the children hated to have to go there to work."

"I can't remember Grandpa doing anything except work," I said. "Wasn't there something he did to relax, something that he just thought of as a fun thing to do?"

Mom's laugh was sharp and pointed. "Just drink on the week-ends," she said. "I guess you could call that his recreation."

"I recall sometimes he would get drunk and the sheriff would just bring him home to the house," Aunt Helen said.

"That's right," Mom said. "If the sheriff found him drunk downtown he would just put him in the car and bring him home."

"Did the sheriff do that for everybody?" I asked. "Especially black people. Did he just pick them up and bring them home?"

"No," my mother said. "He always treated Papa different."

"Why?"

"Just because everybody knew him, I guess. He did work for just about anyone, for all the white people. And one thing about Papa, he was a straight talker. He didn't back down from anyone, black or white."

Well, which was it? I thought irritably. Did he have the grudging respect of white people because he was a black man who stood up straight and refused to be bent by anybody? Or did they think of him as the "good Nigra" who might get a little drunk on the weekend but would work like hell for them during the week?

"Papa was big into the Masons," Aunt Helen said, getting back to the "What did he do for fun?" question.

"He did put a lot of time into that," Mom said. "I remember one time there was a Masons convention and some of the ones who came to town stayed at our house. One of the Masons told Papa that he heard one of the younger members talking about how he liked me. Papa went upstairs and got the man's clothes and threw them down the stairs. Then he kicked the man down the stairs. Told him not to even think about bothering his daughter and put him out of the house."

"One time a member of the Masons came and hid in the house," said Aunt Helen. "Mama would fix food for him and I had to take it upstairs to him. He didn't go out the house for two weeks."

This was the story my Aunt Marie told me earlier, the one I presumed was a case of Grandpa providing refuge to a black man on the run from racists.

"That was down in Florida," Mom said. "I remember that man had killed somebody somehow."

"Didn't the sheriff finally come and get him?" Aunt Helen

asked. "Didn't he just let him go? Took him and put him on a train to somewhere?"

"I don't remember what become of that man," Mom said.

We drove along in silence again, close to Uncle Marvin's house now. I thought about the mysterious Mason—about what he might have done and where he might have gone. What became of him? I wondered. And I wondered if this was another story of Grandpa's softer side that had a hard, hard edge to it.

+⟫━ ━⟪+

The family get-together was like all of our family get-togethers. Everyone brought food that was laid out on a table like a buffet. We lined up to serve ourselves, making sure to take a little of everything so none of the cooks would take offense. There was no table in the house big enough to accommodate everyone. The children were given the playroom, where a cloth had been spread over a pool table for them to sit around it. The older men—most of my uncles and their cousins—sat at the dining room table. Everyone else was on his or her own, left to find seats and use their laps as tables.

In addition to the smorgasbord, these gatherings invariably served up a particular kind of embarrassment for me. There were always people who walked up and just stood there for a moment. Then they asked the question I knew was coming. "You don't know who I am, do you?" When I said I didn't, they would say, "Boy, you ought to be ashamed of yourself. I'm your first cousin!" I will know I'm getting old when someone plays this game with me and ends it by saying, "Boy, you ought to be ashamed of yourself. I'm your brother!"

As soon as I got there, I sought out my Uncle Randolph, the oldest surviving sibling at age seventy-five. Health problems had slowed him in recent years. He walked slowly and needed a cane. But he was quick-witted and talkative. Whenever I asked the other siblings about something they couldn't recall, they said the same thing: Go ask Randolph. "Make sure you don't leave before I get a chance to talk to you," I told him. "I'd like to ask you some questions about Grandpa and the farm."

"I'll tell you anything you want to know," he said, "long as you promise to put it in the paper just like I said it."

I smiled. My relatives always thought my conversations with them were fodder for my newspaper columns.

Uncle Marvin was in a room with a couple of other people watching the Georgia-Kentucky football game on TV. I sat down next to him. I put my plate in my lap and looked for a flat place to put my iced tea—tea so sweet that if you put a string in the glass, sugar crystals would grow on it. The first thing he said to me was, "I'm going to be sixty next year, you know." I knew, but I hadn't thought about it. I knew Uncle Marvin was born the year Grandpa bought the land. And I knew next year would mark sixty years since that event. But I had never put those things together. It was much easier to believe the house would turn sixty next year than it was to believe he would.

I questioned him between plays of the football game. What was Grandpa's relationship with Mr. Cawthon? Was there ever a dispute between the two over land? What color was the house originally?

Uncle Marvin shook his head. "I really don't know," he said. "You should talk to Randolph. He remembers all that stuff."

I got my chance late in the day. I wasn't the only one eager to talk with Uncle Randolph, and my turn came just about last.

"This won't take long, Uncle Randolph," I said.

"That's OK," he said. "I'll answer all the questions you want. You just have to make sure you get it right when you write it."

"Do you remember anything about the house being built?" I asked. "Do you remember anything about the men who worked on the house?"

"I remember one of the men who helped build the house. He was a black man named Rip Upshaw," he said. "But the house was built by Rooks and Sons. Rooks' son was the man in charge. His name was Gene Rooks."

Could the "G" have been for Gene? I wondered. But "Rooks" wasn't close to the last name, whatever it was. "Do you remember anyone named George Mashburn or Mathews or Washburn? I found that name written inside a wall."

Uncle Randolph screwed his face in concentration. "No, I don't recall anyone with a name like that."

"There were some other names, too. 'Rip' was there, and 'Obe' and 'Tweet.' Do any of the others sound familiar?"

"No," he said. "I don't recognize any except Rip. Rip Upshaw is dead now."

"Do you remember what the original color of the house was?"

"It was that brown sort of color. And another thing I recall about them building the house. There was an old house already on the property when Daddy bought it. They used some of the lumber from that house to build the new one." That fit Grandpa's frugality. And it explained the mixture of rough and dressed lumber in the frame.

"What kind of farming did Grandpa do?"

"He grew a lot of cotton at first, and then other things. We also had about twenty cows at one time. They came down with some kind of disease. The vet came out and looked at them and couldn't figure out what was wrong with them. The whole herd got wiped out. And Daddy always had pigs around, too. He was good at putting up meat."

"Did you work in the fields much?"

"Oh, yes. We were out in the fields working, all of us. . . . I don't ever remember going to school for a full term. Daddy would say, 'Such-and-such one can go to school at one time.' Then another one could go in March, and so forth. . . . I really didn't go to school enough to get my lessons. If you got to be older or the biggest one in the class, the teacher would help you out. The teacher was Miss Fannie Henderson. She paddled children in the hand with a stick. She got me one time for fighting at recess. She got me good.

"We used to have to go to work at a place called Buckeye Hill. We didn't like going there to work. We were already tired, and we had to go do some more work at Buckeye Hill. The boys would mostly ride in the wagon with Daddy. But the girls had to walk."

"Do you remember much about Grandpa's involvement in the Masons?"

"Oh, yes. I remember that. He used to keep the Masons' book in a desk in his bedroom. I used to sneak in there and get it out and read it. There wasn't nothing in there that inspired me to be a Mason.

"And there was a Mason showed up at the door one day and asked Daddy to hide him." This is the third telling of this tale, I thought. Uncle Randolph went on: "He had killed two people with a shotgun, but he was a fellow Mason, so Daddy had to help him. The sheriff come and got him a couple of weeks later. I don't remember what happened to him. The sheriff might have been a Mason, too, and let him go. Or he might have taken him straight to jail. I just don't remember exactly."

The story had been spun around to show its most malevolent face yet. The stranger was no longer a fleeing victim of racists. He was a double murderer. In fact, the sheriff's treatment of him— whether he let him go or simply arrested him peacefully and took him to jail—could mean only one thing. The victims, like the shooter, had to be black. If the victims had been white, not even the Masons' oath would have forced a sheriff to afford the man such treatment.

"What do you know about how Grandpa got the money to buy the farm?"

"It was a loan," Uncle Randolph said.

"But I've got a copy of the deed that doesn't say anything about a bank loan. It says Grandpa paid two thousand dollars cash for the land," I said.

Uncle Randolph laughed. "My daddy never had two thousand dollars," he said. "It was a program by the federal government to help provide affordable housing for Negroes. They even gave money for a mule and wagon."

I thought about the old story of all the freed slaves being promised forty acres and a mule. Was this New Deal program a belated fulfillment of that pledge, with the acreage pushed to 103 by inflation in the more than seventy years since Emancipation?

"You were supposed to repay them with the cash you got when you sold your crops," Uncle Randolph continued. "They wouldn't loan you money unless they thought you were a good risk. They just thought Daddy was a good risk and that they would get their money back.

"But you couldn't make money farming back then. On the farm, you could work all year and come up with ten dollars in profit. I remember one time Daddy ended the year with eighty dollars. That was the most he had ever made farming. He asked Mama to put it away for him."

"What was Grandpa's relationship with Mr. Cawthon? Were they friends?"

He looked at me as though the answer to the question was self-evident. "Well," he said, "they were on friendly terms, but I wouldn't say they were friends. It was the same old black-and-white thing back then."

"What did Grandpa and Mr. Cawthon call each other?"

"Daddy always called him 'Mr. Cawthon,' and Cawthon called him 'Jim.' But Daddy didn't mind being called 'Jim.' He'd rather that than being called 'Buddy,' like he was when he was a boy."

"Do you remember Grandpa having a dispute with Mr. Cawthon over land? Did he have any problems with whites in general?"

"No, he never did. One time our cows got out and destroyed another man's crops. The man said he would get the sheriff and let him decide what was fair for Daddy to pay, because the sheriff was impartial. Now, you know the sheriff was white, and he was going to be with the white man."

"How long did you live in the farmhouse before you left?"

"I was around for two or three years. Fred was in Jackson, too. He mostly worked for the Carmichaels, doing little jobs and delivering stuff for them. I remember he drove a brand-new Model-T truck. But Fred left to go to barber school in Atlanta. He had several barber shops up there, but he never made much money. He was fronting for a white man.

"I left to go in the army. Me and Chester was drafted. James joined up on his own. Fred didn't go in because they found something wrong in the physical exam."

"I thought all of you volunteered," I said. "And I could almost swear that I saw a picture of Uncle Fred in an army uniform."

"No. Fred didn't go into the service. James was the oldest, and he was the only one who volunteered to go in. Chester and me was drafted. I didn't want to go. I wanted to stay on the farm. I thought we'd be shooting our rifles as soon as we got out of the boat. But it wasn't like that. When we got overseas, we were playing baseball after a few days. I never was in the fighting as long as I was over there."

"I thought all of you were in combat."

"Not me. James and Chester were. Chester went all over Europe. He was in Italy. One of his assignments was as a guard at the airbase for those black fighter pilots. What do you call them?"

"The Tuskegee Airmen," I said.

"That's right. And James was in combat in the Pacific. He fought at Guadalcanal. I saw him one time when we were both on leave in Australia. I asked him if he was scared while he was fighting. He said, 'Yeah, I was scared as hell.' But I didn't fight when I was in the Pacific, either. I only saw one dead Jap the whole time. He was lying down in a creek, in the water. He had a suit on. A Jap civilian went down and pulled his body out of the creek."

"What was it like when you got home from the war?"

"The first thing was that I got mad with Daddy for selling some of the land to Mr. Cawthon. We were all unhappy about it. He hadn't told nobody about it. And he didn't show us no record of the transaction.

"After I got out of the service, I didn't want to stay on the farm no more." How are you going to keep them down on the farm, I mused. "But I didn't know of anywhere else to go, and Daddy wanted me to help with the work. So I just stayed. But finally, James and Chester came down and sneaked me off the farm, took

me up to Atlanta. Eventually, they did the same thing for
Marvin."

I pictured a sort of an Underground Railroad ferrying the
Fitch boys to freedom.

+⟩━ ━⟨+

The ride down I-75 to take Mom and Aunt Helen home was
mostly silent. Aunt Helen was the most talkative, telling a few
stories about Grandma and Grandpa.

"Mama always stuck by Papa's side," she said. "Even when he
went to work for people, she went along with him to do some
work, too."

"You mean she did housework for them while he did something else?" I asked.

"That's right," Aunt Helen said. "She was just loyal to him."

"Now, Myrtle was the one Mama always counted on," Aunt
Helen went on. "She knew she could depend on you, didn't she,
Myrtle?"

"That's right," Mom said.

"We went through some times back then," Aunt Helen added,
"but the good Lord brought us through."

CHAPTER 15

It was time to pay a visit to Rita Cawthon Kinney. It wouldn't be the social call I should have made months ago, the one I failed to make even after she and her husband graciously dropped by to introduce themselves and wish me well on the house renovation. I wanted to clarify some of the things I had learned about the land. And I wanted someone to tell me her father's side of the story.

I heard a hint of hostility in the way my aunts and uncles spoke about the land transactions between Grandpa and L. H. Cawthon. A strand of suspicion ran through the story, as if everyone felt something not quite right had happened. Uncle Randolph, who had the sharpest memory of that time, sounded particularly vehement and bitter about it. But who was the anger directed toward? Did they think Mr. Cawthon took advantage of Grandpa somehow? Or did they think Grandpa sold the land behind the family's backs, not telling anyone how much money he got or where the money went? But why would a man who got excited about making a profit of eighty dollars for a year of work—so excited, in fact, that he shared the news with his wife and asked her to "put it up" for him—turn secretive about coming into what had to be a large sum of money from the sale of the land?

Something else about Uncle Randolph's story confused me. He said he was upset to learn when he got back from the war that Grandpa had sold the land to Mr. Cawthon. But that would have been in 1946. I thought L. H. Cawthon's first recorded involvement with the land was in 1954. Was Uncle Randolph right when he said there was no record of that transaction? Or was it that the transaction that hadn't been recorded was one that took place in 1939? Perhaps the two men made a deal then that came due when the war ended. Maybe that was what Grandpa didn't want anyone to know about, not even his family.

I wanted to ask Rita about these things. I wasn't looking for a defense of her father. I didn't know that there was anything he needed defending against. What I wanted was information that would help me understand the history of the land—how it came into the family and how so much of it slipped away.

She sounded eager to help when I telephoned and asked if I could come by and talk to her about her father's dealings with my grandfather. "Like I said, I don't know a lot about it," she said. "But I'll tell you what. I'll call my Uncle Porter. He should know all about this. And my brother Harold has all kinds of papers, deeds and stuff like that. I'll see what I can find out before you come over."

We agreed I would drop by on Sunday afternoon after she and Charles got back from church.

The weather that Sunday was as beautiful as it had been the day I met them. But while that first encounter occurred on a day that was an appetizer before spring was served up, this day was a sweet treat before the start of the long fast of winter, which was less than a month away. When I drove up their driveway, I saw evidence of the Kinneys' faith in the promise of all the beautiful days to come. A gazebo had been built just beyond the front yard down toward their pond. Over the last few weeks I had heard the sounds of sawing and hammering that might have been mistaken for echoes of my own work. But it was Rita and Charles's own project, something to give them more time outdoors.

I parked near their carport and walked around to the front

door. I should have known better. As soon as I rang the doorbell, Rita popped around the corner from the carport. "Hi," she said. "Come on around this way. I don't think we've ever used that front door." That's the rule with these ranch-style houses. The front door is usually a formality.

"I see you've got a new gazebo," I said. "Did you have it built?"

"Oh, no," she said. "That's all Charles and me. We've been doing it all ourselves. Every bit of it. And I want to tell you I didn't like being up on that roof putting down shingles."

"It's beautiful. You really did a great job."

"Well, thank you. We think we're going to get a lot of use out of it."

I followed Rita inside. Charles got up from an easy chair and walked across the living room to shake my hand. "It's good to see you again," he said.

"Thanks. It's good to see you," I said. "I was telling Rita how beautiful that gazebo is. She told me you did it all yourselves. Did you buy it in a kit?"

"No. We built it from scratch. When we decided we wanted one I just started looking at different ones and came up with my own design. Then we just went to work building it."

I accepted Rita's offer of a glass of iced tea. I took a sip. It was pleasantly sweet, without nearly the sugar punch the sweetened tea I was used to carried. They invited me into the living room. I sat on a sofa with an ancient child's push car in front of it that served as a planter and coffee table. I put my glass of tea on the doily draped over the hood. We talked some more about gazebos, about the advantages of square layouts over octagonal or round. Then Rita got down to the business at hand.

"Well," she said, "I've got some good news and some bad news. The good news is that I talked to my brother Harold. He's the executor of Bear's estate. Daddy's name was Lewis Cawthon but we all called him 'Bear.' Anyway, Harold has seen all kinds of deeds and other papers that should tell you everything you want to know about that land. The bad news is that all the papers are

tied up while the estate is being probated. Harold says they probably won't be available for at least two months. After that, he said
he'd be happy to give you copies of anything you might be interested in. But right now I can only tell you what he said he
remembers from reading them."

"I'd love to see those papers," I said. "But anything you can
tell me now would be a big help."

"Well, Harold said the land started in your grandfather's family
when the freed slaves were given half land lots, which was about
a hundred acres each."

What? Freed slaves? Half land lots? No one in my family ever
told me anything like that. I interrupted Rita. "Are you sure
about that?" I asked. "I've never heard anything about the land
having anything to do with slavery."

"Harold said it was in one of the deeds. There were all kinds
of notes about the land on those deeds. Wasn't your granddaddy
Mr. Buddy Fitch?"

"Yes. That was him."

"Maybe the land belonged to his father or grandfather first and
was handed down to him. They gave the freed slaves that hundred
acres. Your grandfather's family got some extra land in their allot-
ment some kind of way, because they started out with 113 acres."

"I don't think so," I said. "His family was from Henry County,
as far as I know. They didn't have land in Butts County. Now, my
grandmother's father lived just up the road there. He owned lots of
land, but I don't think Grandpa got any of that. I've got a deed that
shows Grandpa bought the land in 1939, and it was 103 acres."

"Well, Harold says Bear first bought fifty acres from Mr. Fitch
in 1949, and he eventually bought a hundred acres from him in
all. And your grandfather still had thirteen acres left."

Now I was totally confused. "But I thought you said your
father sold land to my grandfather."

"That's not what I said," Rita said. "At least that's not what
I meant."

We were all silent for a moment. Then Rita asked, "Where did
your grandfather get the money to buy the land?"

"I've been told it was a government loan," I said. "One of my uncles said it was from some kind of federal housing program."

"Remember how that house was built straight up and down with no overhang at all on the roof?" Charles asked Rita. "Didn't Bear say that had something to do with an FHA loan?"

"That's right," Rita said. "Daddy said it was a regulation that it had to be that way if the house was built with federal money."

That explained the design flaw that invited moisture damage to the house. But what rationale was there for such a requirement? Had there been some bean-counting bureaucrat who knew a smaller roof would cost a few dollars less, but didn't understand the functions of a roof? Even while the federal government was saving the nation from the Great Depression, it apparently made some very stupid decisions.

I got back to trying to pin down Mr. Cawthon's involvement with the land. "How old was your father when he died?" I asked Rita.

"Bear died January 8 last year," she said. "He would have been seventy-five on January 19."

I did the arithmetic in my head. He would have been seventy-five in 1997, so he was born in 1922, which would have made him seventeen years old in 1939. That meant he couldn't have been involved in Grandpa's purchase of the land, much less orchestrated the whole thing behind the scenes. He would have been twenty-seven in 1949 and probably perfectly capable of buying land from Grandpa. But what about that 1954 exchange of six acres for one dollar?

"Was there anything in the papers about a property line dispute between your father and my grandfather?" I asked.

"First you better tell him about how Bear was about buying land," Charles said with a chuckle.

Rita smiled. "Daddy had a way of buying property that you'd have to call very informal," she said. "In the first place, he was always buying land. He did a little work as a mechanic. He was barely making enough to get by. My mama was always worrying how we were going to make it through. But even then, Bear bought land every chance he got. He was always coming home and telling Mama, 'I got a surprise for you.' And Mama would say, 'Please don't tell me you bought more land. How can we afford it?'"

"And you couldn't get by today with the way Bear bought land back then," Charles added. "These days, you buy some land and you've got to sign papers for everything. You don't just take somebody's word. When Bear bought land, there was a lot of things based on the fact that the two people just trusted each other."

"Yeah," Rita said. "Instead of having a contract, he was liable to get a paper sack and write everything on it. And instead of a survey, he and the other man would just look at the land and step things off. They might say the property goes so many paces from that tree or from the creek. Of course, when they finally did have a survey, they found out they weren't even close. One time they had a property line that cut somebody's LP gas tank in half. When something like that happened, they just got together and figured out how much land they had agreed to and set the true boundaries so each one would come out with the amount of land they bargained for."

That casual approach must have been at play in my grandfather's sale of land to Bear Cawthon. That explained why they had to come back and clear things up in 1954 and set the property lines so Grandpa had the six acres of land they had agreed was still his. And it may explain why Grandpa had no papers to show the family when he sold the land. But what about all that land I remembered my grandfather farming even after he had sold it to Mr. Cawthon? Maybe Jim Wooten was right. Perhaps there was some kind of sharecropping agreement between them, or, at least, an agreement that Grandpa would lease some of the land back from Mr. Cawthon.

"Did your father do any farming?" I asked Rita.

"He did a little farming," she said. "But it was mostly raising beef cattle and hay. He had a business selling meat for a while. And he and his brother Porter were in the LP gas business."

"I remember Cawthon Bros. LP Gas," I said. "We bought

from them when I was growing up."

"Tell him how they got into the gas business, Rita," Charles said.

"Well, it started with a train wreck right at the crossing up the road here. When the train derailed, it dropped a bunch of LP gas tanks. Those tanks just laid there. My Uncle Porter was in the insurance business up in Decatur then, and he wanted to move back down here to live. He and Bear got together and decided they would get into the LP gas business. They told the company that owned the tanks that they would pick them up from around the railroad if they could buy them for a token amount. I think they paid just a few dollars each for them. They gathered up the tanks and moved them all to a lot near the tracks. They had them all tested to make sure they were all right. Then they just went door to door getting people to sign up to buy gas from them. They were in the LP gas business."

This was my grandfather's scavenging on a grand scale. While Grandpa picked up discarded bricks to make a few dollars, the Cawthons pick up discarded gas tanks to form one of the town's most successful businesses.

"I think I've probably taken up enough of your Sunday afternoon," I said.

"Oh, no. You're not taking up our time," Rita said. "I'm sorry I couldn't be more helpful with the things you're trying to find out."

"You've been very helpful. I got a lot of new information. And you gave me some other things to look at."

In saying goodbye, Rita and Charles extracted my promise to come back and see them again, and to bring my sons next time. I knew this wasn't a pro forma invitation. They really meant it, and I really meant that I would come back.

I drove away thinking about how much the Cawthons' versions of events differed from what I had been told growing up. They thought the land had been in my grandfather's family for generations, starting as a reparation for slavery. I had thought my grandfather's purchase of the land was our family's first connection to it, and that this ushered Grandpa into the ranks of landowners. Some of what I thought I knew probably was wrong. There were important details I had known nothing about. This visit left me better informed, and more confused.

⊹━ ━⊹

There was another loose end I wanted to tie up. I hoped I could do it more neatly than I had in trying to put together the saga of the land. I wanted to get more information on Rooks and Sons Contractors, the builders of the farmhouse, according to Uncle Randolph's recollection. I wanted to know more about Gene Rooks, the man who supposedly supervised the house-building crew. And I wanted to identify the mysterious Mr. M, who left his signature inside the wall on what might have been the last piece of siding put on the house.

I went to see Charles Carter in hopes of getting some help. He owned Carter Builders Supply, the largest local building materials company and the one that had been in business the longest. He probably was my best bet as someone who would have known about Rooks and Sons and the carpenters who might have worked for them.

Mr. Carter didn't seem anxious to talk to me when I called and explained what I wanted. "I might be able to tell you a few things," he said. "But I don't know how much time I'll have to talk to you. It might get busy here."

I planned to drop in at the building supply on a Saturday. I told him I would only need a few minutes. If he was busy, I would wait. And anytime he needed to break away to take care of something would be fine. Everything would be done at his convenience. I asked what time would be best for me to come see him.

"We close at twelve on Saturday," he said. "Why don't you come around eleven? I might have some time then."

At 11:00 A.M. sharp I walked through the front door of Carter Builders Supply. There were four men behind the store counter. They were having a leisurely conversation with their lone customer. I walked to the counter and asked for Charles Carter.

"He's in the office back there," one of the men said. "I'll get him for you."

Mr. Carter appeared in a few minutes. He looked to be in his early sixties. His hair was white. We shook hands as I introduced myself.

"How long do you need?" he asked. "I'm going to have to leave here to get to the bank before it closes."

"I just need a few minutes," I assured him. "If I'm not done when you need to leave, you can go right ahead."

He walked me back to a display of kitchen cabinets where there were two stools we could perch on while we talked. I took out my notebook and asked him what he knew about Rooks and Sons.

"I remember it," he said. "E. I. Rooks owned it. They were on the corner of Oak and First streets. You know, across from the jail where the city parking lot is now."

"They built my grandparents' house," I said. "It's that two-story out on Covington Highway before you get to the bridge. I've been told one of the sons was the foreman on the job. Gene Rooks."

"Yeah. I know that house," Carter said. "Rooks did a lot of work around here. The father ran the business. Gene did a lot of the work."

"Do you remember what became of Gene Rooks?"

"Oh, I would guess he's dead by now. I don't know for sure. When E. I. Rooks died, he left the business to Gene. But Gene wasn't a businessman. He didn't run it right. He wasn't aggressive enough to keep customers or something. He could do good work, but he kept losing business to the competition. They went out of business. Last I heard, Gene left town and moved down somewhere in South Georgia. I don't know if he got into the building supply business down there or did something else. I think at one time there was talk about him coming back here, but I don't think he did."

"There's one person who worked on the house who I'm particularly interested in. I want to find out who he was," I said. "Do you know if there was a carpenter named George Mashburn or Washburn or Mathews who might have worked for Rooks and Sons? He would have been working here around 1940."

Carter pursed his lips in concentration and looked up at the ceiling for a moment or two as if the answer might be found there. "Yes," he finally said. "I believe I knew of a carpenter named George Mathews who was around back then. I don't remember much about him though. I might be wrong."

I went from excitement when he said "Yes" to disappointment by the time he reached "I might be wrong." I made one last try at finding a clear trail to follow. "Do you know of anyone who would have been involved in carpentry back then who might remember him?" I asked.

"That was a long time ago," he said. "There aren't many from back then that are still living." He glanced at his watch.

"I better let you go," I said. "I appreciate your help."

"Sorry there wasn't that much I could tell you," he said as we walked toward the door.

"You've been a big help," I said. Then I remembered something else I wanted to ask him. "Can I ask you one more thing? I'm trying to figure out how much the house cost to build. Do you have any idea how much a house that size would have cost back then? Would it have been less than ten thousand dollars?"

He laughed. "No, no. Not nearly that much," he said. "A house like that? Back then it probably cost no more than seven or eight hundred dollars to build it."

+=— —=+

I'm no historian, that's for sure. My search for the history of the house and the land took too many wrong turns, hit too many dead ends. And there's still lots of speculation in the mix I've come up with. No doubt professionals would say my methods of inquiry are inconsistent and ineffective, that I could have gotten more facts and gathered them quicker if I had known more about what's on the public record and where to find it. They would say I relied too little on official documents and too much on unreliable recollections and family lore.

I plead guilty to all those counts. But I add that my goal from the start wasn't just to know the facts. I also wanted to try to know the people involved, whether they were my relatives or others who came in contact with them. I'm far from drawing complete portraits there, either, but I'm far beyond where I started.

What tells me more of what I really want to know, the deed that says Grandpa's purchase of six acres of land he already owned from L. H. Cawthon in 1954 was for the purpose of establishing the true property line between them, or the fact that my mother and her siblings accepted the story that Grandpa in fact did buy the land for one dollar? I say the latter, because it shows what my relatives believed and remembered about those times. It was easy to accept that a deal between a black man and a white man was not always what it appeared to be. In that place and in that time, a lot of what passed between blacks and whites was clandestine.

And the dry deeds recording his land purchases certainly wouldn't have told me nearly enough about what kind of man Bear Cawthon was. No plat or legal description of property drawn up after a survey would show him pacing off the distance from the old oak tree to the big rock over yonder and writing it all down on a scrap of paper. The public record wouldn't show that seller and buyer believed they had an iron-clad deal before the first piece of paper was filed at the courthouse. A handshake was good enough for them. And none of the papers would show that if legally binding words they contained proved to be wrong, if honest mistakes had been made in the transaction, Bear Cawthon was the kind of man who was willing to set things straight and not press any advantage gained on a technicality.

As I said before, I tried to tie things neatly together. The strands of human affairs tend to resist that sort of orderliness. Even when the public record is put in order, all disputes declared legally settled, all obligations and privileges made explicitly clear, the people involved may resist accepting resolution. They may hold grudges, harbor suspicions, and suffer regret. They pass down stories of what happened that favor their perceptions of events. Those stories reveal what people believed and felt. Yes, I want to know the facts. But what people believed and felt—that interests me even more.

Besides, one of the things buying the land and renovating the house has done is to buy me more time to discover the full story. The tale remains open and ongoing. Others will have the opportunity to build on what I've found, because the Fitch family farm isn't history yet.

CHAPTER 16

This daughter of Atlas has got hold of poor unhappy Ulysses, and keeps trying by every kind of blandishment to make him forget his home, so that he is tired of life, and thinks of nothing but how he may once more see the smoke of his own chimneys.

— Homer's *The Odyssey*

The longest quest is the journey home when memory eternally makes home better than the place we are or any place we ever will be. I didn't know exactly what I was looking for when my brother James and I bought the farm. I see now that it was a search for an idyllic history of the Fitch family farm woven from memory and myth. I wanted to find the home I remembered from my childhood. I wanted to find the home I imagined for the generation that came before me. I discovered things that were worse than I ever expected; I found things that were better than I should have hoped for.

I knew my grandfather better than I thought. He really was a man always at work. That was the way people defined him, and apparently how he came to define himself. Jim Fitch worked for just about everybody. That's why just about everybody liked him.

And Jim Fitch worked everybody around him, which meant he worked his children. Oh, how he worked those children! He worked them until they finished everything he had for them to do. Then he worked them some more by selling their labor to someone down the road who had work to do. He worked his children, and he worked his children's children. But he didn't have the hold on the grandchildren that he had on his own. It was a different time and different circumstances by the time he got to us. We depended on him for nothing. We had our parents to thank for that. They made sure we would never have to go through what they went through—never have to go work up on the infamous Buckeye Hill.

What kind of man was my grandfather? The stories I heard on that Saturday at Uncle Marvin's house made me wonder about a man who pushed his children to work into exhaustion and beyond; a man who placed his need for his children's labor ahead of any of their needs, including their need for an education. Did those things make my grandfather a bad man?

Grandpa demanded no more than what he believed he had a right to expect. That surely was no more than had been expected of him when he was a child. It definitely was not as much as he expected of himself.

But what should I have expected as I looked back? And having seen what I saw, who am I to judge my grandfather? I have his tendency toward silence. I am not the warmest person in the world, either. Anyway, like all our traits, human warmth comes in degrees, not absolutes. There is warmth in all of us, and coldness, too. Isn't it likely that my grandfather's heart was full of warmth on that day he came with his mule and wagon to court Julia McKibben?

And if I deign to judge Grandpa, should he be measured by today's standards? His were different times and different conditions. The law didn't compel or expect parents to send their children to school when there was work to be done in the fields. The economic conditions then were worse than anything the people of this country have experienced since. As Ben Hamilton said, people were literally starving to death. People had to scratch and claw just to keep their families together, to even survive.

On what charges would I indict my grandfather? That what he put his children through amounted to exploitation and abuse? He would answer that what he demanded of his children wasn't excessive. He would say it was a necessity. Do I accuse him of being greedy? He would ask how someone who has to work so much to get so little could be charged with greed. Do I label him stingy? He would answer that it's not stinginess to keep what you have when you have next to nothing. How, he would ask, could anyone be called stingy who considered it a good year to end up eighty dollars ahead?

And when I do judge Grandpa harshly, am I being fair? Can I cast a cold eye, look at him objectively, without bias? No, I can't. I hold something against him. I am disappointed, and I blame him.

I wanted to find something different about my grandfather. In the end, the facts got in the way of a good story.

I had hoped for intrigue in Grandpa's purchase of the land. I wanted to find that Grandpa entered into a deal that was supposed to leave him in debt for life, living as a sharecropper or tenant farmer on land he owned only in name. If the story had unfolded as I wished it would, it would have ended with my grandfather beating the system and winding up with land of his own. But that's not the way it happened. It was a straightforward transaction. The man who didn't believe in going into debt did just that. He received a loan from a New Deal program—enough to buy the land from a man named McCord and build himself a house. Bear Cawthon wasn't involved. He was just a teenager then.

When I learned all of that, I asked my mother what she knew about H. H. McCord. "That must have been Mr. Hugh McCord," she said. "Papa used to work for him. Mostly he trained mules for him."

And Grandpa didn't beat the system that discouraged black ownership of land. Those 103 acres didn't put my grandfather among the county's gentry. But he owned the land he lived on, and it was more than a yard and a garden patch. That must have meant something back then. Yet he almost immediately began whittling away at that status. In ten years he had sold most of the land to L. H. Cawthon. The very soil under the Fitch family's feet was sand in an hourglass, steadily draining away over time.

I wanted there to be something unusual about my grandfather's relationship with Mr. Cawthon. But, as Uncle Randolph said, the two men were cordial, but not friends. How could they have been? They were a black man and a white man in the rural South in the 1940s, after all. There was not even the pretense that they were on equal footing. Bear Cawthon was always "Mr. Cawthon"; Grandpa was always "Jim." This despite Grandpa's being older than Mr. Cawthon. He was old enough, in fact, to have been his father. But it was the younger man who received due deference. I do not fault Mr. Cawthon for his superiority in the relationship, no more than I fault my grandfather for his subservience. For their interactions to have been conducted any differently back then would have been not just unusual, but unimaginable.

And, most of all, I wanted to unravel all the layers of weathered and work-toughened skin that covered my image of my grandfather like an onion's. I wanted to find a soft core of hidden love that drove him. I wanted him to be a man who loved his family deeply, but simply didn't know how to express it. I wanted that unspoken love to be the guiding principle of all his labors, and I wanted his pushing of his children to work to be a corollary to that principle. But I can't say he was that kind of man. He wasn't driven to work so he could give to others or even to have for himself. It seems to me that what drove him more than anything was the fear of doing without. Can there be any doubt that he had to struggle mightily to hold onto the land? Had he not been willing to work as hard as he worked, had he been unwilling to take his children into the fields with him, he never would have gotten the loan for the land. But even his willingness to work from sun to sun and to find any other odd jobs he could had not been enough. He sold the very thing he worked so hard to keep.

But the caveat I always heard about him holds true. He provided for his family. There were men who couldn't or wouldn't do that much, men who had all of Grandpa's faults and none of his virtues. He shouldered his responsibilities, and stood up straight doing it. He gained respect in the community. He was a deacon in the church and was known as a reliable man. Whatever their reasons, whites gave him respect, after a fashion.

So, did that make my grandfather a good man? I believe he was as good a man as he knew how to be. He did good deeds during his life. The help he gave Ben Hamilton's family showed an impulse toward generosity. There must have been other examples.

He must have given his children something more than a tolerance for manual labor. Whether or not they fled from him, they left his house prepared to face whatever life put in front of them. Maybe he toughened them. Or maybe he sharpened their desire to do better for themselves. Whatever he did, he did not break them. Perhaps he simply showed them how not to be broken.

Grandpa died in 1968. He was seventy-four years old. Death came while he was in the house and in bed. It seemed an inappropriate way for this man to leave a life spent almost entirely outdoors and at work. Maybe it was just time for him to rest, at last. My memories of events surrounding his passing are hazy. I remember not feeling as sad as I thought I should. I remember the funeral, with a string of men getting up from "Amen Corner"— that set of pews to the left of the pulpit where the deacons sat— to deliver eulogies. Some called him "Deacon Fitch," some "Brother Fitch," and some "Mister Buddy." They said good things about him: that he was hardworking; that he was always willing to donate his labor for some church project; that he was a man you could count on; that he raised a family that anyone would be proud to have. A couple of the Fitch siblings were very emotional, crying, calling out "Papa! Papa!" But I remember most of them being silent and grim-faced, as if they were making an effort to hold something inside themselves. It must have been a great sadness of some kind.

James Washington Fitch left the land and the house as the locus for three generations of the Fitch family. He bought the land and had the house built. He worked from sun to sun to make it a farm. He could be distant and domineering, but he sowed the seeds of

a close-knit family. There were summers when they were all
drawn back—James and Chester from New York; Betsy from
McDonough; Marie, Marvin, Fred, and Randolph from Atlanta;
Doris from wherever her husband's Army career took them; and
Myrtle and Helen, still living in Jackson, less than two miles away.
They all came back. They brought their children. They told stories. They laughed, and even as they laughed, they must have been
constantly confronted with reminders of things they wanted to
forget. But they came back anyway. They came back because this
was home. This was, after all, their family place.

⊹⊱━⊰⊹

I learned nothing during this journey that changed my feelings
about Grandma. She was the softer side of a hard life. But there
was a toughness beneath that sweet gentleness. There had to be.
She was the protector in the household. She protected her children as best she could, showing them that there was more to life
than labor. She grew more assertive and more protective of her
grandchildren, enforcing her own set of child labor laws. ("Papa,
you're about to work those children to death," she would say.
"They can't stay in the field in this hot sun. They're not used to
it.") And she protected Grandpa from himself—hiding those
truck keys and ushering him to bed.

   Late in her life, Grandma once told me she didn't want to go
into the hospital for any reason. "Once you get my age, if you go
in you don't come out," she said. She did go into the hospital
when she was ninety-three years old and ill. She died there. I'm
sure she would have rather had the end come at home, where she
tended the indoor potted plants that had become her garden. I felt
a deep and abiding sadness when she died. The funeral was held
on a day of light but steady rain. It seemed the whole world was
crying over the loss. Grandma used to say, "Don't send flowers to
my funeral. Give me my flowers while I can still smell them." But
there were many bouquets and floral arrangements sent for her.

Someone read the cards ("With sympathy to the family" . . . "In loving memory of . . ."), said who they were from, and held the flowers high so the congregation could see them all the way to the back. It looked as if they were offering them up toward heaven so Julia Fitch could have a good look at them, too.

By the time James and I bought the farm six years after Grandma's death, the beautiful flowers and bushes she once watered by the dipper full had gone to seed or died. But one spring day, while I was working in the front yard, I spotted a flash of pink in a clump of weeds. I looked closer. A rose bush was pushing itself up. There was only one blossom on the bush, and it was the kind of flower you'd want to give to someone you love. There were buds promising to deliver more. I decided to nurse the bush along and try to grow a bouquet. I watered it and put plant food down for it. But I was away from the farm for a couple of weeks. There had been no rain, so by the time I returned the rose bush had withered and lost its flowers.

It was remarkable that the rose bush had appeared at all after so many years of neglect. I considered it a gift from Grandma. She had put enough love into that plant to keep it coming back until I came back, no longer the little boy who trampled her flowers playing baseball in the front yard. I came back a grownup who could appreciate that miracle she helped produce.

I'm not an assiduous record keeper. Far from it. I'm the guy who makes manufacturer's rebates worthwhile for the companies that offer them. I buy the product with the full intention of getting that enticing refund of part of the purchase price. But, inevitably, as the deadline for claiming the rebate approaches, I find myself frantically trying to figure out where that receipt went. "I saw it right on top of that pile of papers on the floor the other day," I moan. "Where could it have gone?"

So, it should be no surprise that I can't lay my hand on every receipt for everything that went into the work on the farm. I don't know how much I spent on nails or tools or paint brushes or paint. But I do have documents for the big-ticket items, starting with Jim Gann's ninety-seven-hundred-dollar bill for fixing the foundation, to the six-thousand-dollar contract for the new siding. By tallying those kinds of major expenses and adding conservative guesstimates for the minor ones, I come up with more than thirty thousand dollars put into work on the farmhouse. I have no doubt that that is many times more than the total Grandpa paid for the house, plus everything my grandparents paid for repairs and additions in the years they lived in it.

I worked on the house steadily for twenty months. (So much for my original estimate that my work would be done in six months. Contractors have nothing on me when it comes to stretching a job.) By my reckoning, I put in more than twenty-five hundred hours in the house hammering and sawing, tearing down and building up, doing and redoing repairs. I was there during the schizophrenic weather reign of El Niño, sweating through record-high summer heat, shivering through record-low winter cold.

Through it all, I was warned by well-meaning people that I was spending too much money, too much time, and too much energy on the house. They asked me what I was getting out of it. I couldn't give them a precise answer to that question then. Now I can.

What have I gotten out of my investment of money and time and work in the house? Much more than I put in.

I learned a lot.

I learned about home repairs the way an avalanche victim learns about snow. I was buried in the work. Some of the people who were hired to help me dig out shoveled more on top of me instead. I had never been afraid to take on renovation or repair projects of a certain scale, jobs that were plotted out step by step in how-to books. While working on the house, I learned to go far beyond that. I learned the value of soaking up knowledge while working alongside someone who knows how to do something. I learned to look at projects as journeys with a starting point and destination. What needed to be done was whatever got me from one point to the other. Forethought would show me the shortest route; flexibility would allow me to negotiate the detours without losing my way.

I learned a little about the Zen of carpentry while studying at the feet of the master, Ben Hamilton. I can't hold an unmarked board with one hand and make a power saw sing and glide along the surface to cut an unerringly straight line. But I can hold the saw steadily and make it drone along as it follows a pencil-marked line. That's a start. I can't walk across a steeply pitched roof carrying a sheet of plywood on a windy day. But Ben has taught me that it is possible. I understand the concept: leverage and balance in all things.

I have learned more about people in their various permutations. They change from moment to moment and in the long term. There is more to them than they show; there is more to them than we see. On the continuum of human behavior, things have a way of balancing out. An Austin may beguile you with smooth talk, but a Ted Watkins will come through for you with quiet hard work. Maybe you get pushed beyond frustration by a contractor who won't come back to finish work you paid him for a week ago, but then a Ben Hamilton will show up and offer his help in repayment for a good deed done fifty years ago.

I learned about the lives of those people who came to this place before me—my grandparents, my mother, my aunts and uncles. I gained a deeper appreciation for what they endured in their lives, and for what they did to ensure that my life would be better. They rose up through stifling racial oppression. They worked hard. They coped with the economic deprivation of the Great Depression. They survived the horrors of a world at war. They did not complain. My generation owes them debts that will never be repaid. So, too, will generations to come.

And I learned some things about myself. I have more patience than I thought, if I can be patient enough to let patience kick in. I can get into too much of a hurry to get anything done. I can work with my hands, and I need to. I can find happiness in the small things. My memory is sharp and selective. I inherited my grandfather's stubbornness about getting things done, but not his infinite capacity to work at doing them. I have my grandmother's love of beautiful plants, but not her ability to coax them into full bloom. My search for the father I never had continues even as I learn to be the father I ought to be.

＋＝⯈ ⯇＝＋

The farmhouse remains a work in progress. Even so, it has been transformed. I doubt Grandma and Grandpa would recognize it. The color of the new siding, according to the brochure, is "Everest"—a light blue-gray that's a lot more lively than the dull brown of the original. The house has so many things that it didn't have while they lived there, from the foundation to the new roof. The small back porch has been replaced by a large dining room. They started with no bathrooms and added one almost thirty years later. Now there are two. Rooms have been divided, walls have been moved, and closets have been added. My grandparents relied on the tight fit of the tongue-and-groove board interior walls to keep the cold wind outside and the heat inside during the winter. Now there's insulation inside the walls and insulated glass in the windows. Fire once crackled in wood-burning stoves and in the fireplace to heat the house in winter. Windows were raised to create a cross breeze to help cool it in summer. Now a heat pump hums year-round, heating in winter, cooling in summer.

And the work on the house earned the county inspector's stamp of approval. I have only Ben Hamilton to thank for that.

I've spoken about the house as if I have a doctor-patient relationship with it. I have, in a way, even though I don't claim to be a house doctor. I just know that in making repairs and improvements my goals have been to cure the house's illnesses, mend its wounds, and inoculate it against future ailments. The physician's first obligation is to do no harm. I hope the things I've done to the house fulfill that duty.

I call the changes I've made in the house "improvements." Does that mean it's a better house now? By today's standards, by the codes and regulations that measure the livability of houses, yes, it is better. But as Dan Curl told me early on, the house has served the purposes for which it was built. It has changed over the years to do that. I hope to enable it to do so for many years to come.

I've discovered many things I didn't know about the house. I know now that Rooks and Sons Contractors built the house, and that Gene Rooks, son of E. I., oversaw the work. What I learned about Gene Rooks is sketchy, but that may be just as well. That allows me to fill in the unfinished portrait as I please. Charles Carter says the company went out of business after Gene Rooks inherited it. I take that to mean he was a craftsman at heart, not a businessman.

The house has not given up all of its mysteries, of course. The identity of "Mr. M" remains elusive. I know for sure that the names inside the wall are not mere graffiti. They are the signatures of men who worked on the house. Rip Upshaw and others left word that they were there. But the questions remain about "Mr. M." Why was his name, alone, placed higher in the house than the others? The others printed their names. He wrote his in a frustratingly inde-cipherable cursive scrawl. Why did he do that? Who was he? I con-tinue to pursue answers, but finding them may be left to my sons. To make it easier for them, I've not covered that signature in insu-lation and Sheetrock. Instead, clear plexiglass allows anyone to take a look at that signature and try to figure out what it says.

Work on the land has barely begun. Perhaps an acre has been cleared of knee-high grass, weeds, and brush. The front yard awaits someone with my grandmother's touch. In the back, the kudzu has been beaten back only a little. That aggressive vine still claims most of the territory. But when winter comes, when the plants have gone dormant and the snakes and other critters are in hibernation, I plan an all-out attack. Catch the kudzu napping and wipe it out.

And what then? What happens when the house is furnished

and ready for someone to move in, and when the land is cleared? I'm not sure. I don't think I can reestablish the family's agrarian roots. My attempt to conquer five overgrown acres with my twenty-horsepower garden tractor pales in comparison to Grandpa's cultivation of 103 acres with a one-mulepower plow. I still call it 'the farm,' but I don't expect to make it one again.

But I hope I can let this place do for others what it has done for me. I hope it will be a place where our far-flung family can gather to celebrate the good times or to comfort each other in the bad times. I hope it will be a place where children will make memories they carry with them for the rest of their lives. I hope that, in the end, this won't be so much about ensuring that the land always belongs to us, as it is about ensuring that we always belong to the land.

ACKNOWLEDGMENTS

Everyone has an idea for a book. But getting beyond that easy act of conception and through the hard labor in which books are born requires that others believe in the idea. I consider myself fortunate to have encountered such people. I offer thanks for their help.

First, I thank Chuck Perry, president and editor of Longstreet Press, for believing that the story of my grandparents' farm was worth putting into print. More and more, it seems, being in the business of publishing books with the expectation that people will buy and read them is an act of faith. When a first-time author like me is involved, it is an act of blind faith. I hope there always will be people like Chuck who keep the faith.

John Yow, my editor at Longstreet, also put his faith in me. He never lost it, despite having reason to do so. I am grateful for his steely patience and gentle guidance. There were times when I felt lost on the path to finishing the book. John showed me the way.

My projection of how long it would take to write this book was as overly optimistic as my schedule for renovating the farmhouse. Thus, thanks should go to colleagues at the *Atlanta Constitution* for allowing me time off from work. Ron Martin, editor of the *Journal-Constitution*, and my boss, Cynthia Tucker, editor of the *Constitution* editorial pages, graciously granted the leave time I needed. Fellow board members Marilyn Geewax, Jay Bookman, Joe Geshwiler, and Maureen Downey took up the slack in my absence. I know that making up for the loss of my production was a light load, indeed, but thanks anyway, guys.

I owe a special "thank you" to another *AJC* colleague. Benita Dodd applied her considerable copy-editing skills to a first draft of the manuscript. She probably saved John Yow some work and without doubt saved me much embarrassment. She went beyond catching spelling, grammar, and punctuation errors to offer substantive suggestions that made this a better book than it otherwise would have been.

I doubt the book's narrative does justice to Ben Hamilton's contribution to the work on the house, but I hope it at least comes close. Ben also was generous in sharing his childhood memories of Butts County and in explaining home renovation techniques. Ben, your debt to my grandfather has been repaid many times over.

Buying the farm would not have been possible without my brother James's assistance; renovating it would not have been possible without his indulgence of my dream. My other brothers, Julius and Fred, also lent their labor and encouragement, as did my sister Patricia. Even dedicating this book to my mother does not adequately recognize her contributions, so, thanks again, Mom. Thanks also to my aunts, uncles, and other relatives who over the years shared their stories of my grandparents and the farm.

Finally, and most importantly, I thank my family for their support and understanding. To my sons Joakim, Gabriel, and Steven: Thanks for being forgiving beyond your years for all the time with you I missed while working on the house and the book— the baseball, basketball, and soccer; the pizza parties and bike rides; the weekend trips and all the rest. And thanks to Claire for being there for the boys when I wasn't. Quite simply, I couldn't have written this book without each of you.